WHAT PEOPLE ARE SAYING

Most retirement books deal with either financial planning or choosing a new locale. Neither of these topics, however, will secure a successful retirement. In *Solving the Retirement Puzzle*, Peter Lindquist takes a more holistic approach. He discusses freedom, new challenges, financial issues, changes, health (physical, mental, and spiritual), relationships, and self-esteem. He concludes with solutions to the retirement puzzle. The approach is solid and the advice, well-reasoned. This book is well worth the time invested in reading it. There are enough salient issues and questions to hone anyone's direction as he or she implements a retirement plan.

—MARY HELEN and SHUFORD SMITH
Authors of *The Retirement Sourcebook*
and *101 Secrets for a Great Retirement*

I read *Solving the Retirement Puzzle* three times and found my puzzle of adapting to a new life solved. The lives of so many people are beautifully told and reading these helped to make my life easier to understand and accept. The observations at the end of the chapters bring into focus some things I had never thought about. I am sure that this book will be very helpful to people who are trying to adjust to retirement.

—PEGGY BECKER

This book is a valuable resource because it tells the stories of how real people adapted to important issues that all of us face when we retire. The stories are engaging and well written. Peter Lindquist has an excellent grasp of the issues and a wonderful ear for the purpose, humor, and wisdom of his respondents.

—ROBERT ATCHLEY, PhD
Author, *Continuity and Adaptation in Aging*

The book serves up a wonderful menu of ideas and personal experiences— very nicely and sensitively written. You come away with at least a half dozen really good thoughts that apply to your own situation. That's what I thought was good about it. There is no one answer. Everybody is different. And this book helps you come to grips with the issues that are meaningful to you.

—JOHN HILL

Solving the Retirement Puzzle is an interesting blend of light reading (short personal case studies) and heavy philosophical discussions (meaning of life issues). I thoroughly enjoyed reading about other people's approaches to retirement and their attitudes toward the final third of their lives. The book is well written and very insightful!

—JANE LILLYDAHL, PhD

Beyond a certain age, life's biggest challenge is growing gracefully. Retirement is dangerously deceptive: it sounds so easy, but reality shows it is stunningly difficult. Many people, perhaps most, fail retirement in one aspect or another. This readable book can serve as a guide, an inspiration, and a road map for your own retirement. Don't grow old without reading it.

—RICHARD D. LAMM
Former Governor of Colorado

My favorite part about the book was reading about the people! There were so many of them that had such inspirational stories and were so full of wisdom. It made me want to seek them out and get to know them better.

—BRAD BICKHAM, CFA, CFP

SOLVING
THE
RETIREMENT
PUZZLE

*How to get the most
out of the rest of your life*

J. Peter Lindquist

MOONLIGHT

Lafayette, Colorado

Printed in the United States of America
10 9 8 7 6 5 4 3 2 1

International Standard Book Number: ISBN 0-9723422-2-2
Library of Congress Cataloging-in-Publication Data applied for.

For more information about Life Puzzles,
go to www.lifepuzzles.org

Moonlight Publishing LLC
2528 Lexington Street
Lafayette, CO 80026 USA
www.moonlight-publishing.com

Cover and text design by Boulder Bookworks

To laugh often and much;
To win the respect of intelligent people
and the affection of children;
To earn the appreciation of honest critics
and endure the betrayal of false friends;
To appreciate beauty;
To find the best in others;
To leave the world a bit better,
whether by a healthy child,
a garden patch or a redeemed social condition;
To know even one life
has breathed easier because you have lived.
This is to have succeeded.

RALPH WALDO EMERSON

CONTENTS

Introduction

(Why a book about retirement?)

AFTER WORK, I would often go home and collapse on the couch with a book or magazine. It was one of my favorite ways to relax during my transition from the workday back into my personal life. The day I retired from the company I had founded eighteen years earlier, I did the same thing; but instead of relaxing I was blind-sided by a startling realization. My company didn't need me anymore! In fact, my associates could survive quite well without me. The jolting questions were: Could I survive without them? What would be my new driving force? What would be my reason for getting up off that couch?

Like a lot of people, I had been immersed in my work. There were always missions to accomplish, lists of things to do. I had prided myself in doing them well and on time, and the rewards had been substantial. But now I was facing a new unknown. I had not planned my retirement. And I wasn't quite sure how to operate in this unfamiliar, amorphous space.

The more I thought about it, the more questions surfaced. What would I do with all my newfound time? How would I

1

replace the stimulation and competitive juices that had, until then, come from my work? Since my work had largely defined who I was, who would I become now that it was gone? Would my wife, Gayla, and I tire of spending so much more time together? Would we each have to sacrifice some of our independence and privacy? And on!

It seemed that the answers to these questions would determine whether retirement would become an exciting new chapter in my life or a dreary ending to it. It also occurred to me that I probably wasn't the only person asking these questions.

A little research was in order. I read several books about retirement, but they didn't answer my most perplexing questions. So, I started interviewing people about their retirement experiences and the lessons they had learned. This led to more research, more interviews and ultimately, to this book.

I learned a lot, even more than I expected. I found that people generally do find happiness in retirement and that they do so in myriad ways. The people I talked with confirmed Napoleon Hill's observation that "Happiness is found in doing, not merely in possessing." But I also discovered that over the course of their retirement years, many people want more than just happiness. For them, sitting back and watching the world go by is not an option, and playing endless rounds of golf is not enough. They want to be mentally stimulated. They want to be fulfilled. They want their lives to have meaning and purpose. In short, they want to make sure they get the most out of the rest of their lives.

In this book, *retirement* is defined as the post-career period of life during which most of us can live our lives as we choose. A *successful retirement* is a retirement in which we achieve the level of long-lasting happiness and fulfillment we desire. *Happiness* is a state of joy and well-being. And *fulfillment* is a state of satisfaction that is achieved when we are proud of ourselves, are committed to personal growth, and know that our lives have value.

As part of my research, I interviewed more than one hundred people with widely different backgrounds—I call them the Retirement Puzzle Cohort. From these interviews, I selected the forty mini-biographies in this book.

Among other things, the comments from the people in the cohort show that vocational achievement does not necessarily lead to a successful retirement. In fact, career-focused people often have difficulties with the transition. However, most of the people I talked with have been able to make their retirement years rich and rewarding. In *Solving the Retirement Puzzle*, they relate how they have addressed their most troublesome retirement questions, including:

- How to be sure that it is time to retire

- How to successfully convert from a high-intensity work life to an unstructured retirement life

- How to deal with changing relationships with husbands, wives, and adult children

- How to live with mates compatibly and still have independence and privacy

- How to avoid "going through the motions" and experiencing day after day of mind-numbing sameness

- How to prepare financially and avoid financial pitfalls

- How to work and retire at the same time

- How to remain mentally alert and aware while many contemporaries falter

- How to address the problems associated with deteriorating physical health

- How to protect self-esteem during the aging process

The curious thing about these questions is that the answers differ from person to person and from couple to couple. The people in the Retirement Puzzle Cohort didn't always agree with one another, because what works for one person does not necessarily work for another. So it makes sense to learn about how different people have lived their retirement lives—how they have solved their own retirement puzzles. My observations at the end of each chapter point out common threads, but it is important to remember that while we all face similar challenges, we each have to discover our own solutions.

Solving the Retirement Puzzle is for achievement-oriented people who want their retirement experience to go beyond happiness to fulfillment. It does not simply concentrate on financial planning because there are so many other books that do just that. The focus, instead, is on overcoming the expected and unexpected challenges that retirement brings. I suggest you make some notes as you read—blank pages are provided at the back of the book—because the people from the Retirement Puzzle Cohort provide hundreds of ideas, many of which could change your life. The goal is to help you solve your retirement puzzle and get the most out of the rest of your life.

ONE

Liberation!

(Now what? How should we approach retirement?)

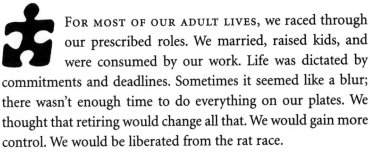 FOR MOST OF OUR ADULT LIVES, we raced through our prescribed roles. We married, raised kids, and were consumed by our work. Life was dictated by commitments and deadlines. Sometimes it seemed like a blur; there wasn't enough time to do everything on our plates. We thought that retiring would change all that. We would gain more control. We would be liberated from the rat race.

Not so fast. What we tend to forget is that our families and careers have shaped our aspirations, our values, and the pace at which we live our lives. We are products of our past. Our families and careers have helped define who we are and what we do. And we don't radically change on the first day of retirement. In fact, many of us will initially experience more frustration than relief as our fast-paced lives crash pell-mell into an absence of focus and activities. We have to shift gears, and a period of adjustment is required. Over time changes will come, if only because the kids have grown up, the intense jobs have been left behind, and there is a new life to explore.

For some people the prospect of change brings joy, for others anxiety. Both emotions are justified because the future will produce both opportunities and challenges. Other people and circumstances beyond our control will inevitably affect our lives.

In this chapter, we meet five people who are thoroughly enjoying retirement in totally different ways. Assessing what they have in common leads to some preliminary conclusions about what each of us can do to achieve the happiness and fulfillment we seek.

Dave Mitchell – *The Joy of Living*

DAVE MITCHELL LOVES LIFE — because he has discovered how to bring happiness into almost every day. Dave was an inventor and businessman who retired about five years ago. Now in his sixties, he starts most days with a simple question: "What do I want to do today?" He then moves on to live out his daily wish, which may mean working on his race car, searching for companies to license his patents, visiting friends, making tools in his machine shop, reading to kids, riding his bike, gardening, spending time with his grown sons, taking an ethnic cooking class, working out at his health club, making jelly, or doing whatever else happens to come to mind.

In Dave's words, "My life is not ideal for me every day, but almost every day. Most days, something will strike me and I will say to myself, 'God, I love my life' or 'Boy, I'm really enjoying what I am doing right now.' I say it out loud or I say it quietly. Before I retired, I liked life okay, but I am happier now than I have ever been. It's not even close. I always knew that there was so much more out there — that my life was much narrower than I wanted it to be. I was working and I was raising kids, but there were so many things I really wanted to be doing that I wasn't. Now I am doing those things, and I know that next week, or next month, or next year I will be doing something that I have never done before. I'm just not sure what that is yet."

As wide as his interests are, Dave also knows what he wants to avoid. "Pretty much, if I don't enjoy it, I don't do it. If I don't enjoy it, I have somebody else do it." He likes to keep what he calls the "have-to" projects to a minimum. He may have to go to the grocery store or cut the lawn, but he doesn't have to do it today or tomorrow. The workweek does not get in his way. The one "have-to" that he relishes is reading to vision-impaired kids. "On Tuesday mornings, I have to go read to my kids. I enjoy being with them. I get a kid on either side of me on the couch and usually they're snuggling against me before the session is over." He doesn't view this activity as an obligation or responsibility. "I never thought about it as 'giving back.' The satisfaction I am getting is that they enjoy it. And if they enjoy it, I enjoy it."

Dave also enjoys traveling, which he does throughout the year. During racing season, he goes to car races around the country. And in the last two years he has assisted an aging professor, his mentor when he was younger, on trips to the Cayman Islands and Italy. This was a way to return a favor to someone who meant a great deal to Dave and who helped shape his life.

These trips required some planning, which is an anathema to Dave's free-flowing lifestyle. Like many other creative people, Dave likes to live and think spontaneously. "Schedules don't work for me. I'll take the risk that I might not get a room, and sometimes there's a downside to that. But I'd rather be a 'free spirit' so that I can do whatever I want, whenever I want to do it." This lifestyle is easier for Dave when he travels than it would be for many others because he has good friends all around the country. There are few places he goes where he does not reconnect with people he knows and enjoys.

During his working life, Dave invented and patented brakes for in-line skates. (Think of how many kids' bones were not broken because of Dave!) He also received patents on technology that allows sailboats to sail more efficiently into the wind. In retirement, he keeps his creative bent alive by building custom items for himself and friends. He loves the challenge of designing new things.

In fact, he loves the challenge of exploring almost anything new. He can't understand how anyone would not share that perspective. "I was having lunch with a friend, and he said something about how he didn't want to live too long because he thought he would be bored, and my reaction was, 'How can you ever get bored?' Maybe, if I was ninety-five and in a wheelchair. Maybe, I'd be bored. But I don't think so. I can't imagine being bored. There's too much to do. I have days when I get irritated because there is so much to do."

One time, Dave told a wealthy doctor friend about his morning routine. "It just got to him when I told him that I wake up in the morning and ask myself, 'What do I want to do today?' As a result of that comment, the doctor realized that his own life was out of control. He was working too hard. He was too busy to have fun. He was blowing his one opportunity to live his life the way he wanted. In a matter of a few months, the doctor sold his practice and set out to do what was important and rewarding to him."

Dave's life is full, and he has no regrets about how he is living it. In the midst of all of the joy that he has discovered, he has one lament. "I know that I will someday die not having done everything that I would like to have done. I'm not going to get uptight about that. It's just a fact, because there are just too many things to do."

Shari Ulrich — *What is Success?*

SHARI ULRICH EXUDES POSITIVE ENERGY and curiosity. Her interests are wide-ranging, and she finds joy and satisfaction in learning as much as possible about each of them. This desire to learn and grow has carried her through her career and into retirement.

When she was a sophomore in high school, Shari wanted to become either a flight attendant or a psychologist. She ended up doing both. After graduating from college as a Phi Beta Kappa with a bachelor's degree in psychology, she became a flight attendant with TWA. She was enthralled. The people, the crews, the international travel—they all added up to fun, excitement, and a perpetual learning experience. She had originally planned to quit after a few years and go back to graduate school. Instead, she decided to continue her flying career.

However, since flying did not fulfill her need for intellectual challenge, she elected to go back to school between flights. Over the ensuing years, she earned one more bachelor's degree, three master's degrees, and a Ph.D. in psychology from Johns Hopkins University. "I always led a double life. I didn't suffer any. I studied overlooking the Acropolis. My life has been enriched by it. I found such joy in being a flight attendant, but it was partly because I had sufficient intellectual stimulation elsewhere."

Shari's unique career path allowed her to live and study in Europe, as well as in several major cities in the United States. "After getting out of college I think my reference for success changed a lot. I was told not to become a flight attendant. 'Go to graduate school, go to medical school … be successful!' But I was determined to fly. I loved it, all twenty-three years. I found that it was more important to listen to my heart than to do something that answered to someone else's, or society's, definition of success. And that has held me in good stead all of my life. I also think that over time I learned to use the 'life energy' that I have in other interesting ways, not expending it on things that have little meaning for me."

After completing her career as a flight attendant, Shari utilized her training in psychology by becoming a victim's advocate with the Colorado State Patrol. The work was demanding and consuming. Among other things, it included advising families when their loved ones died in traffic accidents and then counseling them during the traumatic aftermath. Calls for her services could come at any hour of the day or night. Later, she trained other staff members to provide these services. Understandably, the job took its toll.

She and her husband, Kurt, retired to the mountains. Now approaching sixty, she manages her extended family, one dog, two cats, two llamas, and the herds of deer that frequent their 480-acre ranch. Shari, however, does not comfortably admit to being retired. "The word retirement has a negative connotation to me because it sounds like you are closing doors." That is about the last thing she is willing to do, and she would probably accept another job if she found the opportunity sufficiently interesting and challenging.

In the meantime, Shari pursues new opportunities for which there previously had never been enough time. Her interests include playing the cello, practicing archery, becoming a pilot (she would also like to fly helicopters), playing the piano, reading, and studying German. "When experiences start repeating themselves over and over again, then it's just not as interesting anymore—because it's like you've reached a plateau. To me there are so many reasons to be alive and to value what your opportunities are. I just think: go, go, go."

She also loves being involved in other ways. "I think that exchanging stimulating ideas as we grow older is crucial. But so is humor. That is just one reason why it is important to get out and be engaged with other people. I love to laugh really hard, and when there are just two of us on a ranch in the middle of nowhere, we don't always have that opportunity. My humor usually revolves around human experiences, spontaneous plays on words, observing humorous things when no one knows I am there, or just seeing how different people view the world. So it's important to me to stay involved with other people.

Shari has her own ideas about what is necessary for a successful retirement. "You may have a lot of money, and you may have the idea that retirement is rest and relaxation, but if you're interested in life, that probably won't be enough. People have to have interests that pull them forward. Those interests might not have a lot of meaning for other people, but they should have great meaning for the individual."

Shari's life remains full because she identifies activities that interest her and then commits herself to becoming proficient in them. She has learned from the past but does not dwell in it. Her focus is on experiences that will take her to new levels of knowledge and enjoyment. "It's always nice to be around people who are excited about life and what they do—and who are challenged by it."

Clark Ewald –
Renegotiating How to Live Together

CLARK WAS RAISED IN MINNEAPOLIS and graduated with a mechanical engineering degree from the University of Minnesota. For thirty-five years, he worked for Public Service Company (now Xcel Energy, the fourth largest electricity and natural gas energy company in the U.S.), ending his career as the senior vice president in charge of the customer organization. He has been retired for nine years.

"My dad's career was always extremely important to him—and to my mother. For some reason, I didn't get as wrapped up in mine. Early in my career, my job didn't dominate my life the way it did for my dad and lot of other guys. It was something I did and I liked it, but Martha and I always had a lot of other interests. We traveled a lot. For twenty-five years we took motorcycle tours with friends. We had cabins and skied, and I played golf. So, there were a lot of diversions.

"Near the end my career, my job required a lot more time. We had thirteen district managers with great teams. And one of the joys of my job was being able to go out and visit them and do reviews. But I was putting in sixty-hour weeks, and I was totally exhausted. So, while the last few years were enjoyable and rewarding, they were a little rough. By the end I'd had it! I was working hard, and the environment was changing. We had a retirement plan that allowed me to retire with no reduction in benefits when my age and years of service added up to ninety-five years. So, I retired three months before I turned sixty.

"I think that it is extremely important to come to peace with your career, with that chapter of your life. If you can't say at the end of that time that you are comfortable with what you did, if you can't get that door shut, if you haven't achieved what you set out to achieve, or if you feel something is lacking, you are going to have problems. You have to do that before you can move on." This was not an issue for Clark. "I think I made the transition into retirement by the third stoplight on the way home from work on my last day. It went very smoothly."

Nevertheless, there were some transitional issues that he and Martha had to face. "We made a deal up-front that we weren't going to constrain each other, that we would both continue to lead our own lives. And we have done that. I have not tried to organize her spice rack. We each have our own space. I stay out of the kitchen, and she stays out of the shop. But one of the surprises about the transition has been the importance of negotiating a new relationship. There very definitely is a period of time when a couple has to renegotiate how they are going to live together. Before they retire, couples are separated for about twelve hours a day. They each have their own lives. They're doing their own things. Then all of a sudden there are two bodies banging around the house at the same time. I think there was some blindness on my part about what my wife had to go through. I was self-centered and focused on my transition, and after a while I realized that I wasn't the only one in transition.

"We traveled a lot, especially at the beginning. And the travel prevented her from some of the things she was used to doing. She couldn't take the pottery classes she wanted because we were gone so much. We missed several of the conversational German classes we had signed up for. Our friends ended up with more of our symphony tickets than we did because we were gone. So I was taking her away from her life and what she wanted to do. The biggest problem was that I didn't appreciate what it meant for her. I don't think we had any huge issues. It was just recognizing that it was a big change for both of us.

"At first, we were going to build a new home in the country for our retirement, but the area where we bought our property was being developed and ended up looking like it was in town. Then we looked at townhouses. But they were more expensive, and we would have less space and would have to give up some of our privacy. So, finally we looked at the changes we could make to our existing home to meet our needs. It all started with Martha saying, 'I need a bigger refrigerator.' We ended up pushing out walls and expanding the kitchen, and now we're happy as larks. One of the pieces of advice that I give people now is, 'Retirement is a big enough change by itself. Do that first and give it some time before you decide to pack up and move. You quit working. You change your whole life environment. You leave your friends. That is way too much to do all at once.'

"As I got closer to retirement, I started to make a list of all the things I wanted to do. I have always been interested in photography, and I've fiddled around with it all my life. I envisioned myself as a great landscape photographer, and I bought a Hasselblad camera with a couple of lenses and all the special gear that goes with it. Then, I took a seminar from John Fielder, who is a marvelous landscape photographer. His whole theme is that light, not the mechanics of the camera, is the key to photography. He talked about how the contrast is minimal at the first light of day, and that's when you get the best photographs. So he would plan his shots the night before and get up in the middle of the night to be set up for the shots when the sun came up. I thought, 'Somehow this isn't going to work for me!'

"The other thing I did was take up the piano. I had no musical training, but I have loved music all my life and have enjoyed listening to classical music. My wife is a great pianist, and I always had thought I'd really like to learn how to play. So I started playing when I retired, and I've been at it nine years. I spend a lot of time at it, and it's very enjoyable because you *can* learn the piano. It's very slow and very tough, but you actually can see some progress.

"Another thing I thought I was going to do was read more, because when I was working everything I read was work-related. I read all day long, but there was so much more I wanted to learn about. So I subscribed to *Foreign Affairs, The Washington Post* Sunday edition, *The Economist, The Wall Street Journal,* and several others. But all they did was pile up. I didn't get them read because I found out I just didn't want to sit down and do it. Other things turned out to be more interesting to me. So I don't think that people necessarily know when they retire what they will find most interesting.

"I've also been busy serving on some boards of directors. Because my job involved contacting all of the communities we served, I was always on a lot of boards. But after I retired I realized that in many cases I was just there because I was representing the company. So I resigned from those boards. I kept a few board positions, and those have kept me interested and active. But you have to decide if you are really making a contribution or if you are there for some other reason.

"I think I had my eyes open when I started retirement. If I had any concern, it was that I wasn't sure that I had enough to keep me busy. But I don't think that I have been bored for two hours since I retired. Once in a while I'm stuck with an hour between appointments or activities, but I have not experienced just sitting around and wondering what I am going to do with myself. I tell people who are retiring not to worry. You get up in the morning with nothing to do and at bedtime you're only half done. Don't worry about it!"

Marilyn Haas – *Changing with the Times*

SINCE HER FATHER WAS A RAILROADER, Marilyn Haas's family moved frequently. The pace continued after she married Barry, and he became a sales representative for Alcoa. During one eighteen-year period, they moved eleven times. Between moves, she found time to have four kids and a string of different jobs: a retail sales rep, a fabric rep, a women's clothing store manager, and the executive director of a merchants and property owners association.

Through it all, she became adept at managing change and balancing the various roles she was playing. Still, balancing everything was sometimes a chore. "There were some things that I missed, particularly with the last two boys. I tried not to, and I was fortunate because my schedule was usually flexible. Doug, the youngest, would probably tell you that he was at my mercy more than the others, because I had him doing more chores than he liked for downtown activities and events. But everything worked out pretty well. We all survived."

Marilyn retired in 2001, but Barry kept working. Initially there was a period of adjustment. "In the beginning I had some issues. Suddenly, I was home alone. It was so quiet, and I was used to being really active and involved. I found myself running back and forth to town because my life wasn't at home. I wanted to stay in touch with all the people who I had been associating with through my work. That got to be real tiring. After a while I started to do more at home. Then Barry's mother got sick and we moved her. That took up a lot of my time for a year. After that, we bought and started fixing up another house."

Marilyn has also been involved in several volunteer activities. "I am on the Imagine Foundation Board. It is probably one of the most meaningful boards I have ever been on. The Foundation works to help people who were born with disabilities, like Down's syndrome or autism, and it has a wonderful children's program. I get a lot of satisfaction. We have gotten some tax support, but it never seems to be enough to take care of all the cases that are out there. There are people who have been on the waiting list for one of the group homes for more than ten years. It is so hard on the families.

"I am also on the board at the history museum. That's a hands-on thing that I love because I love history so much, and I love preserving the community. In fact, the one thing that I miss is working on the downtown database. I started it in 1989, and it tracks the property changes taking place in our town. The business improvement district hired me to keep it up-to-date, and that was really fun because I was able to talk to people from all over. I am also involved with a couple of the programs through our church. I love being active.

"I am really enjoying myself these days. You know, what I like the best is that most of my time is spent volunteering. I am not being paid, and so I can say 'No.' And I finally am learning to say 'No,' which I have never done very well. I have always felt obligated. But now I have better control over how I spend my time than I ever did before. When Barry and I were both working, I sometimes thought our lives were parallel. We were on separate paths. We were too independent. So, I really treasure those times when we do get away together. And now that I am not working, if he has to go on a business trip I can go along. It's great!"

One issue that Marilyn is particularly sensitive to is health. "I do worry about our health because there is a lot I want to do while we are able, and you never know when that will change. We have had two kids with cancer. One of our sons had bone cancer a long time ago, when he was twenty-three. Before surgery, he had to sign a paper authorizing the doctors to amputate his arm if necessary. That was tough. Fortunately, he had a bone transplant and they didn't have to amputate. He is in pretty good shape now. Then, five years ago our daughter had surgery to remove a tumor and two lymph nodes. She still has some cancer cells. So now she's getting radiation treatment again. It's hard on her, hard on everybody. But let me tell you, that is when faith really matters. Our faith is what has gotten us through all of this."

Marilyn has learned that maternal instincts do not fade with age. "I think the hardest thing for me has been letting go, letting our kids be adults and make their own decisions. It is hard when they make mistakes. You want to get involved. You want to help out, and you were always able to do that before. But now you have to force yourself to be quiet. Let it be. Even though our kids are all over thirty, I struggle a bit with that."

While Marilyn has found that life in retirement is not free from concerns, she recognizes that it is a time of great potential. "To be happy, I just think that you have to be involved. In my case, I like to be involved in the community. But that doesn't have to be the choice for everyone. You have to find what works for you. If you like to sew, join a sewing group. If you like to write, then write. Just find out what it is that is important to you and follow up with it. And if it is something new, that you have never done before, that's all the better. I don't think you want to get caught in that trap of always saying to yourself, 'I've been there and done that.' Stay involved and explore new things. To me, that's the key to being happy in retirement.

"I also think that it is important to have a positive attitude and not be critical of others, particularly family members. There are people who are too serious. That doesn't mean that you should ignore serious problems, but you have to have fun with life."

David Jackson – *Getting More Out of Life*

Most of David Jackson's working life was in the field of education. After serving two years in the military during the Korean War and teaching for seven years, he became the headmaster of two private schools, first in California and later in New Mexico. Then he became the administrator of a school near Santa Fe for children with learning disabilities. As he approached fifty and he and his wife, Karen, were soon to become empty nesters, he went through a period of life-changing introspection. He asked himself, "What do I really know about life?"

Looking back, David realized that he had spent most of his adult years with relatively affluent upper-middle class people. He didn't have a good appreciation of the human condition in the broader sense, and he felt that he would be shortchanging himself if he didn't gain a better understanding of the world. He and Karen moved to Chicago where he managed a day shelter in the innercity. "One of the things that drove me to work in Chicago was the understanding and appreciation that eighty to ninety percent of the world's humanity live in downright poverty. In Chicago, I got to experience the poor in that setting, and when Karen and I traveled through India we saw incredible poverty. It was quite a revelation and put everything in a more realistic perspective."

About the time they moved to Chicago, David had another inspiring thought. "I read an article in a magazine in which a man had made a list of all of the things he wanted to do before the final bell rang. And I thought, 'I wonder what it's like to farm, to fish for a living, and to work a freight train.'" He came up with an idea that would further expand his horizons. Each year he would do something to make that year special, something to make it stand out against all the others. Typically, it would be a summertime adventure designed to remove him from his familiar surroundings so that he could learn about how other people worked and lived their lives. "All of the experiences were predicated on the assumption that this wouldn't be a normal tourist thing. This would be something different. I wanted to see things from the bottom up."

In the ensuing years, David worked on a farm, traveled on a Mississippi River barge, learned about mining in West Virginia, spent a week with a traveling circus, took a freighter from the West Coast to Korea, studied the timber industry, worked on a deep sea fishing boat, spent time on the streets of Mobile, Alabama, walked the Oregon Coast, picked peaches in the south, lived with the Hutterites and Amish, learned about freight trains, hiked from coast to coast in England, and traveled through Canada and Alaska. The adventures brought great satisfaction and enriched his life. "These experiences taught me a good deal about myself and gave me a better understanding about the breadth of human capacities. It was a very affirming point of view that I gained, very reassuring."

The excursions started before David retired and have carried on well into his retirement years. They have given a unique life to each year and have prevented the years from melding together. He looks back with great satisfaction. "The more I live, the more I read, the more I learn from people about their lives, the more I come to appreciate that life isn't so much about getting 'there'—wherever that is. It's about living it.

"One of the great things about retirement is that you can back off and develop some perspective. You're no longer in the forest.

I think, 'Isn't this incredible? We don't know why we're here on earth or where we're going and very little else of consequence. But it's important to go for it anyway!' I keep a little sign in my study that says, 'Do it now.'

"In my case, my retirement years have been driven by an increasingly lively curiosity about all sorts of things and a desire to broaden my experiences to a point where I could sense something of the spectrum of human activity. And personal reflection is an important aspect of that. I have found that the periods of time alone are immensely helpful in giving me understanding and motivating me."

In addition to his annual excursions, David has been very active in his church, provided career counseling through the YWCA, written a column for his local newspaper, and regularly worked out at his health club. But now, as he approaches his mid-seventies and after more than fifteen of his major escapades, David is finding that his energy for such demanding experiences is beginning to wane. Although they are becoming less frequent, he is delighted that he has learned to know the wider world. "You want to end up saying, 'I'm glad I did' rather than 'I wish I had.'"

Observations about How to Approach Retirement

DAVE, SHARI, CLARK, MARILYN, AND DAVID have different backgrounds, interests, and lifestyles. But since they all are enjoying happy and fulfilling retirement experiences, it is more important to consider what they have in common.

Frankly, they start with some natural advantages that not everyone shares. They are bright, well-adjusted people with strong relationships and good communication skills. They do not have any major health or financial problems. These factors have been shown to be good predictors of a successful retirement.

However, let's look beyond their natural advantages to see what they have done to achieve happiness and fulfillment. By listening carefully to each of them, we find that they have instilled within themselves three critically important qualities. They are adaptable. They are positive. They are involved. Together, these qualities help form a self-assuring mindset that influences how they view themselves and the world around them. Beyond that, these qualities lead to an approach to retirement that is likely to produce happiness and fulfillment.

ADAPTABILITY

In figuring out how to approach retirement, we should understand what we are sacrificing when we leave our full-time jobs. For most people, work is the requisite path to the American Dream. It is through work that many of us find stimulation, satisfaction, happiness, independence, status, power, financial achievement, and fulfillment. As a result, our jobs are often an integral part of our identities. "Who we are" is largely determined by what we do and how well we do it. And the decision to leave that job and retire is recognition that an important chapter of our lives has come to an end.

Thus, for many of us retirement means that a new identity must be adopted. To move forward and find happiness and fulfillment, we must let go of the past and redefine ourselves. We have to adjust to a new reality. We have to separate who we are from what we did. For some of us, this is very difficult.

The importance of adaptability, however, extends well beyond the initial transition. Throughout retirement, we will experience numerous changes that may affect our financial circumstances, health, relationships, and self-esteem. The ability to adapt to these changes will largely determine the level of personal satisfaction that we are able to maintain. So the importance of adaptability does not decline during our retirement years.

We can see from the short biographies that Dave, Shari, Clark, Marilyn, and David define themselves in terms that transcend their previous jobs. Their vitality stems from their values and current interests. They are not bound to the past. In short, they are who they are today, not what they did yesterday. This exemplifies the adaptability that helps lead them to happiness and fulfillment.

POSITIVENESS

As will be demonstrated throughout this book, a positive attitude is an important predictor of a successful retirement. Positive energy leads to more happiness, greater social acceptance, increased productivity, stronger personal relationships, higher income, better health, and extended longevity. Positive attitudes affect who we are, what we do, and how we feel.

All five people in this chapter have positive attitudes. They have self-confidence, a passion for living, and a desire to live life to the fullest. They believe that their lives have been productive. They enjoy living in the present and are working to build a better future. They have confidence in their relationships. They all have a sense of humor and don't take themselves too seriously. They are realistic about what the future may hold. They love being in charge of their own lives and schedules.

INVOLVEMENT

In the absence of the careers that helped provide us with structure and identity, we need to find new sources of motivation. Our success in retirement will depend largely upon our ability to stay involved. We should identify our greatest interests and focus our energy on them. We should avoid complacency and challenge ourselves to grow and develop. And if we want to get the most out of the rest of our lives, we should continue to contribute to society.

Dave, Shari, Clark, Marilyn, and David are engaged in life. They are interested in the world around them. They live in the present. Each wants to experience and achieve new things. They seek out personal challenges. They find joy in interacting with others and easily meet new people. They have strong family ties and a circle of friends that they care about. They have demonstrated an interest in education and a need for mental stimulation. They continue to make contributions to society and the people who are important to them. All have been willing to help less fortunate people. Their involvement is a crucial part of their approach to retirement and central to their happiness and fulfillment.

SUMMARY

These few interviews suggest that by becoming adaptable, positive, and involved, we can develop an attitudinal foundation for achieving happiness and fulfillment. As will be confirmed in the coming chapters, this approach serves us well throughout the retirement experience. We must recognize, however, that being adaptable, positive, and involved will not ensure a successful retirement. The future holds far too many uncertainties, and there are no guarantees in life. As we tell our kids, life isn't always fair.

In fact, we will have to face several challenges for which many people are unprepared. These are discussed in the next chapter. Some of these challenges will surface immediately, while others will evolve as we move through retirement. Most of the people we meet in Chapter Two have had lengthy retirement experiences, qualifying them to speak about the full range of issues we will confront. Subsequent chapters address the ways in which these challenges can be met and overcome.

TWO

The New World

(A new life brings new challenges.)

RONALD REAGAN ONCE OBSERVED that you know you have reached middle age when you are faced with two temptations and you choose the one that will get you home by nine o'clock. A sequel to his quip is that you know you have reached *old* age when you are faced with the same two temptations and you reject them both so that you can stay home. As we grow older, our interests and our inclinations change. What was once fun and challenging becomes less interesting or too demanding.

For this reason, several authors have concluded that retirement is divided into three phases. During the initial phase, we typically are in good health, are charged with pent-up energy, and have unfulfilled dreams to pursue. In this active phase, the pace of our lives may approach or even exceed the pace we maintained prior to retirement. We are "on the go" and are constantly crossing things off our lists. After a period of time, however, many of us will want to slow down. This may be because our earlier dreams have been fulfilled, our energy has declined, or certain health limitations have surfaced. We enter a second, more passive phase, a period of reduced activity. But that does not mean that our minds start to languish or that we cease to have an interest in personal growth. This phase is often characterized by more introspection, and it lasts until deteriorating health and related age issues become so prevalent that they dominate our daily lives, severely restricting our mobility and capacity to carry out daily tasks. At that point we enter

the third phase, during which we may require assisted-living arrangements.

The transition from each phase to the next is usually gradual, and not everyone will experience all three phases. Because of disabilities or illnesses, some of us will enter retirement in the third phase. Some who are in the active phase will meet an untimely end before entering the second phase. Retirement planning should account for the fact that life is not predictable. In any event, our goals and needs will change over time, and we should plan accordingly.

The people we met in Chapter One are all in the active phase of retirement. However, after ten years of retirement and entering his mid-seventies, David recognizes that he is beginning to shift gears. "I have backed off a bit now, and I may be switching into a more passive stage. I'm not worried about whether I am meeting anybody's expectations. I'm moving from being interested in external things to focusing more on inner peace. Doing that is contingent on health and sufficient financial stability and having my personal life in good order. But I am very comfortable. I am where I want to be."

David's observation is important because it demonstrates that moving through the various retirement phases does not necessarily mean a decline in life satisfaction or enjoyment. Happiness and fulfillment can be realized in each phase. However, there will be challenges. Some of the challenges start before

we begin retirement. Others appear later. The six people we
meet in this chapter help us identify them.

Denis Nock – *Staying Charged*

DENIS NOCK IS A SELF-CONFESSED WORKAHOLIC who has
succeeded at virtually everything he has tried—except retirement! During his career, Denis was a stockbroker, operated and
sold a small manufacturing company, headed the corporate
finance department of an investment banking firm, and was a
senior vice president of the Medical Products Group at Bristol-
Myers Squibb. He was also the president of Valleylab when it
went public and, later, when it was sold to Pfizer Inc. He and his
family were financially secure before he was fifty. He had the
option of early retirement and the chance to pursue whatever
he wanted.

He chose to continue working, but with a whole new twist.
His goal was to have fun and give something back to his community. He headed the Chamber of Commerce in Boulder,
Colorado, for seven years. Then, he moved over to direct the
entrepreneurship program at the University of Colorado's
College of Business for five years. "When I went to the Chamber,
working to make money was over. It didn't make any difference
what they paid me. The motivation was different. It was the fun
of building the organization and working with all of the volunteers to figure out how to overcome the problems we faced. In
the entrepreneurship program, it was setting high expectations
and going for it. I love building things."

Finally, Denis retired. Three days later, he set up an office
away from his home as a base for his new activities. He expected
that his involvement with non-profit organizations would keep
him stimulated. "I was on thirteen different non-profit boards. I
thought that was going to be my primary 'thing' and that it

would keep me busy and engaged in the community. But I learned fairly quickly that while non-profit board involvement worked well as a side bar or diversion from my full-time job, attending non-profit board meetings as a primary retirement focus was simply not as satisfying or as fulfilling as I hoped it would be. It probably would have been different if I had been more deeply involved with just a few of them. But I didn't feel like I was making much of a contribution just sitting in board meetings. So I got out of that mode pretty quickly. Now, I'm down to only three of those boards."

In fact, his full-time retirement lasted only fifteen months. "I assumed that I would stay retired, but I wasn't doing very well at it. I just wasn't mentally stimulated enough. I'm a firm believer that you either use it or lose it. When you're working, you go a hundred miles an hour. That's just your natural routine. And then you retire and you slow way down. My metabolism slowed down, I wasn't as sharp, and it was scary. I was worried about not being stimulated in retirement, and it was a problem for me. It's not a problem for everybody, but it was in my case. I now know that the next time I stop working I'd better have something I can get my teeth into."

After his short attempt at retirement, Denis went back to work on a part-time basis analyzing equities for a small wealth management firm, completing a circle back to his investment banking roots. "I love investments and research, and I'm learning. There is no topic or subject that is of more interest to me. I don't have anything to do with running this business or hiring or firing or making decisions. I am very involved in doing the things I want to be doing. I make investment recommendations and am involved in the investment committee meetings. I love working with the bright, young guys. I just can't wait to get to the office every morning. The key is that I am thinking all the time. That's the difference. I've got this little note pad beside my chair at home, and there's not a night that goes by that I don't write down 'X' number of ideas. Whereas during those fifteen months I wasn't working, that pen just sat there."

Obviously, Denis has a need to be involved, but his part-time schedule is perfect for this stage of his life. "I'm half-time, flex-time. We have a beautiful home in Colorado and another in Tucson. During the winter months, we spend ten days to two weeks here and then go to Tucson for ten days to two weeks. The flexibility gives me a lot more time to spend with my family and grandkids than I have ever had before. I absolutely love it."

For the foreseeable future, Denis does not plan to make any changes. "I'm still learning every day, and I love that. If I get to the point where I'm just cranking stuff out without the passion, that will be a big-time signal to me. But I'm not going to retire and just play golf. I'm a lousy golfer anyway. It just doesn't turn me on. I have to do something to keep my mind active. And that means more than just reading. It's creative thinking or scheming or plotting. Like in investment banking. It's trying to do the impossible deal, or trying to do something different or better than anyone else can do it.

"I don't have a lot of things that I want to do when I retire again. That's the whole issue. I mean, when you're a workaholic and you're totally immersed and absorbed in your work, you don't have time to develop hobbies or other interests. You don't even want to. You're just so totally obsessed. Am I a less healthy person because of it? Possibly. But we are who we are.

"We went on a cruise. Actually, I just went along. It was nice and all that. We were on the upper deck, but it was still pretty confining. Being away from the newspapers. Being away from the news. Being out of touch. No stock quotes. It just killed me. Just killed me! Finally, the first time I got off the boat I said, 'I've just got to find a *Wall Street Journal* or log onto the Internet and find out what's going on.'"

Don't look for Denis on your next cruise. He's busy. "I just dread the day when I am no longer stimulated—just going through the motions and 'living life out' so to speak. I'll do everything I can to avoid that day as long as I can."

Bill Fischer – *The Perils of Retirement*

BILL FISCHER IS ANOTHER WORKAHOLIC who had difficulty with the transition into retirement. Bill started with the federal government as a civil servant in 1957. During the Jimmy Carter administration he held political appointments as Assistant Secretary of Energy and Assistant Secretary of Education. Later, he became the executive vice president of Brandeis University and chief financial officer at Northwestern University. The work was always intense and required long hours. As was the case with Denis Nock, Bill's wife was largely responsible for raising their children.

Like Denis, Bill's first retirement effort was unsuccessful. "I retired in 1997 and was retired for eleven months. But I hadn't figured out what that meant, and I was not a happy camper." After a short period back in college administration, his second attempt at retirement succeeded because he had developed a better understanding of the issues involved. "Nobody ever has the full answer to this problem, but I am a much happier guy and more fully occupied. And it turns out that that's the answer—at least for me. I've got to say that there are lots of advantages to retirement, but the key is staying charged and interacting. That's the whole deal. Retirement is more fun than working, but you do have to work at it. You have to be thoughtful about it. You have to think about what it is that will give you happiness and satisfaction."

Because of his first unsuccessful retirement experience, Bill spent a lot of time thinking about retirement, identifying the problems people face, and working through the solutions. In Bill's view, there are several perils that need to be addressed. "The first peril, for someone coming out of a high-pressure, highly charged environment, is that all of a sudden the plug is pulled. The flywheel is still going, all the machinery is still going, but there is nothing to apply the energy to. So, you have got to figure out where you're going to apply this energy. I learned that the only thing that really makes me happy is being a part of something that is bigger than I am. It has to be something that is bigger and more lasting and, preferably, perpetual. If it is perpetual, and it's interesting, and it contributes to society, then I'm happy.

"It doesn't matter how big or small the job is. I drive for Meals On Wheels. I'm just a little cog in the Meals On Wheels program, but it's really satisfying. I don't want to be the manager. I just want to deliver hot food to people who need it, and I have a great time doing that.

"There is another peril for people like me. My wife and I have been married for fifty years, but our lives were always separate. I developed habit patterns that helped me cope in a high-pressure environment, and she developed habit patterns that helped her cope in a much different situation. Now we're under the same roof, more or less, twenty-four hours a day. Both of our situations have radically changed. It is a challenge for both of us, figuring out how to understand each other in a way that we never did before. I'm still working at it. I'll always be working at it. We'll never get this completely resolved. It's a challenge, and you really can't think about it before you retire because there's no way you can understand it.

"My definition of marriage is 'an unlimited stream of accommodations.' That's the only way it works. It has to be coupled with a lot of love and compassion. You're not even going to want to accommodate if you don't have that. But if you have that desire, it's an unlimited stream of accommodations. Some couples may think that they have solved all of their problems by the time they retire, but some of the problems are just starting. And you have to be willing to accommodate each other."

The third peril Bill identified was the aging process itself. "As we get older, it's a little bit like adolescence. In adolescence, you're on this ascent trajectory, and it's not linear. It's logarithmic and it's not uniform. It would be nice if it was a constant upward curve, but it's jagged. Well, I think the later years are the same thing, except it's a descending trajectory. It also is jagged and is not matched for both husband and wife. Human beings do not age in parallel. As we get older we get less flexible — physically, mentally, and emotionally. As we do, we need more support, and some people need it sooner than others."

Bill's fourth peril is the threat of irrelevancy. "In retirement, you become less relevant to your society and what is going on around you. I anticipated it, and it's not hard for me to deal with because I have always felt that the magnitude of your impact on society is not nearly as important as the quality of your impact on society. So, when I deliver Meals On Wheels I don't just deliver the meals. I try to cheer the person up. I try to give something extra. I take the time to find out how they are and what they need. The thing we don't want to do is take people's independence away, if we can avoid it. That's what I meant by quality, and that's how I deal with the peril of irrelevancy."

In addition to driving for Meals On Wheels, Bill is on the boards of his alma mater and a retirement community, where he conducts in-reach programs. He also has a laundry list of other challenges to pursue. "Before I retired, I drew up a list of some thirty-five things I wanted to do that I had never had a chance to do. I've chipped away at it, taking things off the top and adding things to the bottom."

One of Bill's favorite activities is Rotary International. It is another way for him to give something back. "People ask me, 'What religion are you?' and I say, 'I'm a Rotarian' because Rotary has so many advantages. It doesn't own any real estate, so we don't waste all that money. It does a lot of good stuff. It's a structured outlet for doing good things. It's tremendous. I have the time to go to the meetings, the programs are good, and there is no doctrine. It's perfect!"

Carol Grever – *Rebuilding a Life*

CAROL GREVER and her husband, Jim, graduated from Phillips University, a small, conservative Christian college in Oklahoma. Carol became a college professor in English and Jim a college administrator. After several years, they felt that they needed a change, and in 1973 they purchased a near-bankrupt employment agency. As she remembers, "We were partners from the very beginning; it was just a mom-and-pop operation. I did the marketing, selling, and most of the interacting with people. He was good at systems, operations, accounting, and all of the back-office stuff.

"In 1976, we started a temporary-help agency as a separate business. It was so much fun to start something from scratch. The temporary-help industry was pretty new then, and we had to learn the business as we grew. We even had to teach our clients how to use us. By 1980, we understood the business well enough to take on some new partners and franchise our methods. Within ten years, we had 200 offices across the country. But in 1990 Jim and I were really restless in the partnership. So we decided to sell our share to the other partners and just manage the five offices that we owned separately."

By that time, Carol had turned fifty and her two sons were adults. She and Jim had been married for thirty years. She had always planned to retire in her mid-fifties, and her life was pretty much on course. But she was in for the rudest of awakenings. "In 1991, Jim came out to me that he was gay. I plunged into a totally unexpected crisis. Once we know the truth, we can never go back to ignorance."

As it turned out, since early in their marriage Jim had been living a double life. During most of the year, he was a responsible husband, father, business owner, and church professional. But when he traveled away from home his homosexuality emerged, and he lived the life of an anonymous gay man. To the extent possible he repressed his guilt, and inexplicably the counselor he was seeing advised him against informing his family.

Carol recalled the anguish she experienced after Jim's revelation. "For a while we kept up this huge front. Then a few very close friends knew. But we had to carry on this façade of the perfect couple and business partners, and we worked together every single day. I was in the closet with him for about a year. It was pure hell. At the time, keeping secrets was the worst thing I had ever been through. But as it turned out it was the only way that we could have done it. We were wonderful business partners. We are still friends. But we couldn't be married. There was no way that that was going to meet my needs, or his."

Jim moved out of their home in 1993, they sold the business in 1994, and their divorce became final in 1996. "The reason that we stayed together as long as we did was that we had to sell our business. Fortunately, we had already sold our interest in the franchise business. But virtually everything we owned, and our careers, and our identities, and our social activities, were all intertwined. It was very difficult to separate who we were. It was the most challenging thing I've ever done."

Entering retirement, Carol had to totally rebuild her life. "I was really confused for a long time. I had to create a new identity, but I wasn't sure how. I'd get up in the morning, and I couldn't figure out what kind of clothes to wear because I didn't know who I was. Clothes are part of our self-image. But the rug had been pulled out from underneath me. Almost everything I had counted on was gone. I still had my spirituality and I still had my children. But I didn't have my career, and I had lost my self-image. I thought, 'If I'm not Jim's wife and I'm not a career woman, who am I?' At first, I think I was running away. I was on five boards. I was in meetings constantly. I'd get sixty emails a day. It was as if I was still in a full-time job. I think a lot of it was that I was afraid to slow down and think about who I was. I was afraid that if I stopped I wouldn't be anybody. It really was an identity crisis.

"I threw myself into two activities. One of them was studying Eastern religions. I was very interested and it met my needs, so I became a Buddhist. The other was working with the Board of Trustees at Naropa University. I made a job of it. I chaired the board for five years."

Carol Grever's book, *My Husband is Gay*, was published in 2001 and was an immediate success. In it she describes how she and twenty-five other women dealt with the crises that resulted when their gay or bisexual husbands came out. Writing the book was cathartic, and the warm reception it received led to an affirmation of who she is. "I need to have a label in my own mind. Who am I? The success of my book helped answer that question. It helped solidify my thinking about what I want to do. Now I know that I'm a writer. It is extremely satisfying. I know that I can do it, I get a feeling of success, and I feel like I am making a contribution."

Carol learned how to deal with the challenge to her identity, which she absolutely had to do to move on in life. "The only way to get over it was to let go and forgive. The women who don't make it, who sink into alcoholism, or substance abuse, or mental illness of some sort, or suicide, are the ones who harbor anger. It's like eating rat poison and expecting the rat to die. You're just poisoning yourself. Fortunately, I really am a positive person, and it wasn't that hard for me to put the anger behind me.

"Now I'm working on a sequel to my first book. It deals with the long-term prospects for people who have gone through this experience. The working title is *Thriving Beyond the Crisis*. The secrets are maintaining an optimistic outlook and looking to a higher power. The people who have nothing to lean on spiritually are really in trouble."

Having survived her crisis, Carol was able to put things in perspective. "I am in the 'calm after the storm.' I went through ten years of extreme stress, from 1991 to 2001. And things finally evened out. But periods of suffering allow us to more fully appreciate the better times. My blood pressure isn't high anymore. I am in a really wonderful space. I have a relationship with a man I love, and he adores me. My mother is well and I am very, very close to her. I have a terrific relationship with my children and grandchildren. My health is good. I feel as if I am on a solid spiritual path. My work feels meaningful. I love my friends. I love my home.

"I'm not afraid of anything. I am financially secure, as secure as anybody can be in these times. We all worry about the world situation, but I still travel, and I am able to do what I want to do. What more could anybody want? I don't know anybody who is as lucky as I am. I feel good about life; I'm just really blessed, and I can't think of anything I would change. I found out how strong I am, how strong my family is, and how important they are to me.

"I believe in divine order. I believe that there is an order to what goes on in our lives. We don't always understand why things happen to us, but every experience is a teacher. When the student is ready, the teacher appears. It comes in different forms, and you may not like that teacher. But you have lessons to learn. So, everything that has happened in the past fifteen years has been a part of my education. I needed those lessons, and I was given those experiences so that I could help others cope. I truly believe that, and it has become my mission. I feel that I have a purpose."

Brad Beeler – *Mixing Money and Souls*

BRAD BEELER GREW UP IN IOWA. After his college education was interrupted by World War II, he graduated from Iowa State University with an engineering degree. In the 1950s, Brad and his brother operated a residential contracting firm and built 150 homes in the Chicago area. The business was successful, but Brad wanted a different lifestyle, one that would give him and his wife, Peg, the freedom to pursue their other interests. He became a real estate appraiser in 1959 and continued in that profession until 1989, when he turned sixty-five, sold his practice, and retired.

"There were so many other things I wanted to do while I was young enough and healthy enough to do them. Peg and I have always enjoyed outdoor activities—tennis, hiking, biking, and snowshoeing. And we have always been very active in our church, the First Presbyterian. It has opened up many opportunities to serve people who are less fortunate. For example, we became involved with the Soup Kitchen and Lamb's Lunch. Hot lunches are offered on Saturdays and Sundays for the homeless. It was quite an eye-opener for me. Naturally, some people among the homeless are there because of difficult circumstances or emergencies in their lives. However, most are homeless by choice. For various reasons, they have decided to let other folks take care of them. It was a big hurdle for me to help feed and clothe people who *could* help themselves. I had to learn to love people unconditionally—because they, too, are God's children. Anyway, Peg and I now enjoy taking our turns buying and preparing food to serve them."

Brad has had many other long-standing interests, including Lions Club, the Christian Businessmen's Committee, helping untrained computer users, skiing, fly-fishing, and tinkering in his workshop. But one activity that he and Peg have been particularly dedicated to was a guidance course called the

Crown Ministries. Through their church, they ran the Crown Ministries program for almost ten years.

"The Crown Ministries is a national, interdenominational program that lasts twelve weeks. It is designed to help people get out of debt and on budget, to find out what money they have coming in and what is going out. Most of the people in the program have credit card debt problems. It's astounding. Many have difficulty just trying to pay their interest expense.

"We have a problem in this country with obesity, and people are always going on diets. Well, the Crown Ministries program helps people get on a financial diet. They need to change their lifestyles. That is very difficult for many people, but what is so interesting is that with very little change they can be much better off. The Crown Ministries program is so effective because it is done in small group settings and has accountability built into it. We are accountable for doing things God's way. The participants first learn where they stand in terms of their debt, and then there are discussions about how to get out of debt. People learn what their weaknesses are, how they can control their spending, and how they can live better lives. Young people who get into this program and start saving in their twenties are so far ahead of the people who don't understand how important this is. As far as finances are concerned, people can't start setting aside money soon enough. In Proverbs, Solomon shared his wisdom when he said, 'Just as the rich rule the poor, so the borrower is servant to the lender.'"

Clearly, Brad has had many activities that have kept him involved during his retirement, and for him the transition to retirement was not a challenge. "It was very, very easy. That is probably because I started thinking about it years earlier. I didn't retire until I was sixty-five, though I originally wanted to retire five or ten years earlier. As it turned out, it was a very good thing that I didn't retire earlier. When I finally did retire, we were much better prepared financially. And when the stock market took its dive a few years ago, we were in a better position to handle it. Not everyone was so fortunate."

Brad believes that there are two questions people should answer before they decide to retire. "First, you have to know that you have the ability to do it. You have to find out where you are financially, prepare a plan to pay off your obligations, and know that you can meet your future needs. That can be a problem because you never know what emergencies you are going to have in the future. But the second question is important too. It involves a personal decision about 'when is enough, enough?' You can keep on working, but is that all there is to life?

"The answer to the first question deals with what you *have to have* for retirement. The answer to the second question deals with what you *want to have*. And that is different for different people. It is a real relief when you get to the point where you can say that you will be able to get along with what you have. But, you and your wife have to be on-track and agree, or else you will have problems that will stretch your relationship."

Even with all of his training and teaching, Brad was not immune when the stock market declined abruptly. Like most everyone else, his retirement accounts took a serious hit. "We had to be realistic and say, 'We will just watch what we spend and be a bit more frugal. We may be pinched a little bit, but we'll be okay.' We sold one of our cars, and we became more cautious about how much money we gave to our kids. That's where a budget becomes so helpful. It doesn't have to be down to the penny. It can just be some general categories that help you keep track of your spending patterns."

The financial pinch is not the only challenge that Brad and Peg have faced during retirement. "Both of us have had some medical problems. Something was bothering me, and I didn't know what it was. I wasn't able to do some of the things I had always done before. It turns out that I had an irregular heart-beat, and now I have a pacemaker that is working well. But in the past year or two, Peg has had some problems with her leg. So, we haven't been able to be as active bicycling or snowshoeing. That's slowed us down a bit. I miss doing the things that we used to do together, but you just have to be thankful for what you can do — and deal with it."

And he has dealt with it. "All in all, my retirement years have been a very happy time of life. Besides the volunteer work and all of our other activities, Peg and I have traveled in the U.S. and abroad. It has been wonderful, and I look forward to many more productive years."

Peggy Becker – *The Indomitable Spirit*

PEGGY BECKER'S LIFE has been dedicated to helping poor children and families overcome the difficulties they face. Her parents were Methodist missionaries, and they instilled in her the passion to make a difference. While her husband — whose parents were also missionaries — was representing the U.S. government and setting up forestry programs in Korea, East Pakistan (now Bangladesh), Chile, and Honduras, Peggy was teaching and establishing programs to better the lives of disad-vantaged people. "I love poor people. They are so intelligent. They know so much. But nobody appreciates them."

Peggy was selected as Woman of the Year in Chile because of her unceasing efforts to improve the lot in life of the Chilean poor. She formed a mothers' club, taught parents about nutri-tion and educational opportunities, facilitated the gift of a house to the YWCA and set up a pre-school in it, headed a U.S. Peace Corps group, established a program for handicapped chil-dren, founded a Boy Scout troop, taught classes at the University in preschool education, helped the Salvation Army, and taught

Sunday school. "I learned so much from being overseas. I found out what was really important to me. I feel that poor people and different nationalities are not accepted like they should be — even in the States. We should all be equal. But in most countries, everything is controlled by the very wealthy. It's terribly unfair."

This problem was especially apparent in Chile. "I started Boy Scouts for the poor children. Can you believe it? In Chile, they wouldn't allow poor children to belong to the Boy Scouts. I went to their headquarters, and they told me that these kids could never fit in. So, with the help of the Peace Corps I started my own troop. They did a wonderful job. I got eighty uniforms sent from my church in the United States. I got CARE to give us sewing machines, and I asked seamstresses to help. We had the mothers altering the uniforms for their kids. But the national group still would not allow them to march in the Chilean Independence Day parade because they did not have the right ties or tie clasps. So, I put an ad in the embassy paper asking people to hire kids in their homes or yards so that they could buy their ties. They ended up getting the ties and marching in the parade. Later, several of them were even sent to the World Jubilee in the United States."

Peggy was not easily deterred when confronted by problems that would overwhelm many others. "The Communists tried to convert my Peace Corps kids. But I had contacts, and I found out what was happening. One of the mothers in the mothers' club said, 'They're having a Communists' meeting at my house tonight, and I'll hide you in the closet.' I went and found out their whole plan. Then, I contacted our ambassador and I told him what had happened. He said, 'I know what you're up against. I know that the situation we have here is very difficult to deal with, but I really hope that you will stay committed and keep up the good work.'"

When the Beckers moved to Honduras, she started all over,

working to better the lives of the people around her. "My husband always told me, 'I grow trees and you grow children.'" In Honduras, she was involved in setting up schools and libraries, providing shoes to poor children, sending teachers to the U.S. for a better education, and personally financing the education of five underprivileged children through college.

Eventually the Beckers returned to the States, where Peggy started a day nursery, formed and served on the staff of an International Center, and organized a program that brought thirty-two Vietnamese people into the country.

Peggy has set an enviable standard. She has schools and libraries named after her in three countries, both of her daughters graduated from college as Phi Beta Kappas, and family members are now in El Congo (formerly Angola), Costa Rica, China, Russia, and Morocco carrying on the family tradition of making a difference.

For Peggy, the transition into retirement was relatively smooth. "We always stayed involved, even after we moved to this retirement community. You can always find something to do, even when you lose the ability to do the things you have always loved so much. One of the best things that has happened is computers. We use ours to stay in contact with our friends from around the world. I am very involved with our church. And I've done a lot of public speaking to help people understand about poverty. I hope it helps change their attitudes. I've always tried to broaden people's horizons.

"I also got involved with an acting program. I was a storyteller talking about how we got shoes for the poor children in Honduras. We dramatized it by showing how the children took off their new shoes when their mothers came to pick them up at school because they didn't want their shoes to get dirty when they went outside."

Peggy's most difficult challenge came when her husband died

after sixty-seven years of marriage. They had shared so much, and the thought of life without him was unbearable. "I struggled terribly. I did a lot of crying, feeling that I couldn't do anything anymore ... that the world was passing me by. I thought that I wanted to die too. But I would never bring it on. I will fight it until the end. Two times I met with a woman who had a Ph.D. in psychology. Just being able to talk to her made me feel like a new person. I told her, 'You have really made a difference in my thinking. You haven't talked about my grief. You haven't talked about the changes in my life. You've talked about things that are stimulating.'

"I think that people can get over the death of a spouse, but it's better if you have the help of somebody who accepts you as you are and who doesn't say 'you need to do this' or 'you need to do that' or 'it's all right to cry.' That isn't what I wanted to hear. After a while, it's not all right to keep on crying. You may be relieving yourself of tension and of the fear that 'I'm no good anymore.' But I don't think that it is helpful in getting you past that stage in your life."

Soon after her husband's death, Peggy faced another major challenge. She broke both of her hips, an exasperating and painful experience. But in typical fashion, she turned a negative into a positive. The hardest thing for her was to be isolated in the Health Care Unit of her retirement community. "In Health Care you may have your physical needs taken care of, but you need more than that. You need to get well and become involved in activities that are stimulating. And that's what I did. A friend and I discussed all of the changes that needed to be made. It stimulated me because I had found something to do. I did my usual thing—I met with people and got their backgrounds. I met with our CEO. Then we had a meeting with the social workers and other interested people. Those seven weeks that I spent in Health Care turned out to be quite stimulating. Instead of being isolated in my room, I was thinking about what we could do to improve the Health Care Unit and trying to do something about it. What is important is being involved in something and feeling that you can still do things.

"It's also fun to think back over my life, but not just to remember occasions. It's fun because I think about: What are my interests? Why did I get involved in this? Why did this not turn out right? What can I still do? It gets me thinking in a positive way."

In the future, we can expect Peggy to retain her positive outlook. "I think that we must be realistic. The bad things in life aren't just going to happen to other people. They can happen to you, but you have to have the right attitude. I may have broken two hips and they may hurt, but they aren't going to keep me from living my life. I'm going to walk without that walker."

Anne Ophelia Dowden – *The World is a Garden*

ANNE OPHELIA DOWDEN is an extraordinary artist. During her career, her botanical illustrations were published in *Life, Natural History, Audubon, House Beautiful* and in twenty books, about half of which she authored. In a catalog prepared for a six-month exhibit honoring her life's work, the Hunt Institute for Botanical Documentation at Carnegie Mellon University described Anne Ophelia as "one of, if not *the,* country's leading botanical artists."

"I knew from the time I was five years old that I was going to be an artist. I never thought of being a botanical artist, but as time went on I decided that I wanted to be a book illustrator. I went to Pittsburgh to the Carnegie Institute of Technology. After I graduated, I moved to New York City in the depths of the Great Depression to seek my fortune. There couldn't have been a worse time. It was very discouraging, but I finally got a teaching job at Pratt Institute.

"I taught at Pratt for a year or two and then founded the Art Department at Manhattanville College. I taught everything from design, drawing, anatomy, and color theory to history of art, history of architecture, and history of early Italian painting. "But with college teaching, you're not there all day long every day. So, I kept up my drawing. A group of us did a mural for the 1934 World's Fair. Later, that group started doing textile designs for drapery fabrics. So, all the time I was teaching I was doing drapery fabric designs at home. All the designs were plant material, but they weren't very realistic.

"In the summers, I would make drawings of plants and wildflowers as reference materials for the textile designs. But as time went on I decided that I was enjoying doing the plant drawings more than the textile designs. And I still had in my mind that I wanted to be an illustrator of books. In 1952, I drew a series of edible wild plants from Michigan that I sold to *Life* magazine. They commissioned two or three other things, and then I did some work for *Natural History* and *Audubon*. From then on, I concentrated on doing plant drawings, which turned out to be very, very rewarding and very satisfying. And in 1960, I was commissioned to do my first book on plants. Before too long I gave up teaching and focused on getting established with the book publishers."

Established she became! Over the next thirty years she would have nineteen more books published. But when she finished her last book at the age of eighty-five she realized she couldn't continue. "I knew I had to stop when I couldn't see the hairs on a honeybee's legs anymore."

In fact, at ninety-five Anne Ophelia finds that without her art and with deteriorating physical capabilities, life is often a burden. "I really try not to think about it, but I'm afraid I don't have a very positive attitude now. I did for most of my life. But now I have a resigned attitude. It's accepting. It seems to me that all I do is accept one frustration after another. Everything seems to be going downhill. Physically. The eyes. Hearing. Walking to the telephone. Just staying alive. Everything takes six times as long. Every household chore that used to be mechanical now takes planning. It takes time and it takes push. Actually, a day with nothing to do is a real pleasure.

"I have lists and lists and lists because I forget everything. Everybody complains about forgetting names. That, I think, is the first thing that people lose. But I am beyond that. I can forget my best friend's name. And I forget other things too. I can read something in the *New York Times* in the evening, and the next morning I don't remember what I read. I call somebody, and I have to write it down immediately or it's gone. It's very frustrating when it's your mind, but the physical aspects of aging are difficult too. I just can't get to everything that has to be done."

Physical and mental impairment can be consuming, but there is more to the story. Anne Ophelia would only discuss these difficulties when asked, and she refuses to dwell on them. Her energies are elsewhere. Her eyes twinkle when she talks about her love for nature, the joys of her youth, exploring fields and learning about plants and animals, the mysteries of symbiosis, the satisfaction she received from her life's work, and the enjoyment she still feels when people admire her art. The smile is genuine and the joy infectious. Even at ninety-five, some happiness can be found.

Anne Ophelia's comments lead to an important insight. We should seek to challenge and stimulate ourselves for as long as we can. We fail ourselves when we are too quick to lose our initiative or live in the past. Yet, in the final phase of our lives, when the tasks of daily living become difficult and new challenges are wholly unrealistic, it is finally time to reminisce, to relive our lives, and bask in the joy of it—without guilt.

Observations about Life's New Challenges

IT IS GENERALLY ACCEPTED that good health and financial security are basic ingredients for a successful retirement. Yet many people who have good health and financial security are unable to find happiness and fulfillment, while others who are less fortunate have found both. Why?

The answer is simple. Success in retirement is not determined by the problems we face. It is determined by how we deal with the problems that we face. Problems are inevitable. Each of us is unable to foresee how our lives will unfold, and life-changing events will often occur when we least expect them. Even when we avoid significant setbacks, our needs and interests will evolve. Thus, our ability to deal with changing circumstances is crucial. People who have had experience successfully adjusting to change and overcoming challenges throughout their lives may be better prepared to react appropriately than those who have not.

While it is true that we cannot foresee all of the problems we will face in retirement, the people in the Retirement Puzzle Cohort helped us identify the five problems that often arise. Our major challenges in retirement are finding the solutions to these five problems. By doing so, we will be well on our way to achieving the lasting happiness and fulfillment we seek.

THE FIRST CHALLENGE: *Preparing Financially*

Most of the people in the Retirement Puzzle Cohort did not have major concerns about their financial security, but they all agreed that entering retirement financially unprepared or mismanaging financial resources during retirement would be unwise and could be devastating. This is one issue that should be addressed well before the decision to retire is made. However, that alone is not enough. As we find in Chapter Three, there are financial concerns that will arise throughout the retirement experience.

THE SECOND CHALLENGE: *Making the Transition*

Like Denis and Bill, many people experience difficulties making the transition from highly focused, intense work lives to unstructured retirement lives. Transitional problems result from forced retirement, lack of planning, unfulfilled career dreams or expectations, the absence of alternative interests, and identity issues. Chapter Four addresses the importance of dealing with the transition properly.

THE THIRD CHALLENGE:
Managing Physical, Mental, and Spiritual Health

Each of us should accept that over time our health will deteriorate. Our third challenge is to avoid a premature decline caused by our own actions or inactions. We need to understand what we can do to strengthen our physical, mental, and spiritual well-being, while at the same time realistically preparing for the future. This is discussed in Chapter Five.

THE FOURTH CHALLENGE: *Revitalizing Relationships*

In retirement, we experience changing relationships with friends, spouses, children, and others. Revitalizing relationships with the important people in our lives is one of the keys to lasting happiness and fulfillment, and it is our fourth challenge. As is discussed in Chapter Six, we need to understand the changes that take place so that we can respond properly.

THE FIFTH CHALLENGE: *Maintaining Self-Esteem*

If we want to have a successful retirement, we must maintain our sense of self-esteem and overcome what Bill Fischer calls the "peril of irrelevance." This fifth challenge is the least discussed of the challenges we face, but it is crucial that we deal with the frustrations associated with aging. This is addressed in Chapter Seven.

COPING BY BEING ADAPTABLE, POSITIVE, AND INVOLVED

In Chapter One, we found that being adaptable, positive, and involved provides an attitudinal foundation for achieving happiness and fulfillment. In this chapter, we learned about the five major challenges we face in retirement. But the comments from Denis, Bill, Carol, Brad, Peggy, and Anne Ophelia also suggest that adaptability, positiveness, and involvement are skills for coping with the problems that we face. These will be more fully explored in the coming chapters, as we analyze the five challenges and uncover their solutions.

THREE

THE FIRST CHALLENGE:
Preparing Financially

(Money can't buy happiness, but poverty can't either.)

 IN RETIREMENT, THERE IS A FINANCIAL FORMULA that applies to almost everyone. It is:

Money = Stress

If we don't have enough money, we will worry about the future and whether things will work out. If we do have enough, we will worry about all of the things that might go wrong. Even if we have more than enough, we will probably worry about what will happen with the money that is left over after our eventual demise.

Make no mistake. The problems associated with having more than enough money pale in comparison to those that arise out of not having enough. The point is that while some sources of stress are reduced in retirement, for most people money is not one of them. "Money equals Stress" is a reality for most of us, and it is one of many reasons that money can't buy happiness.

Yet while money doesn't buy happiness, not having enough money makes happiness much more elusive. Financial security is not the solution to a successful retirement, but it is a step in the right direction. Adequate financial planning and living lifestyles that conform to our financial resources, are keys to achieving that financial security. But as we will see, the complete solution is more involved.

In this chapter, we first meet a retiree who had achieved financial security but lost it shortly after entering retirement. The implications were disastrous. Then, we talk to two highly successful financial planners who share much of the knowledge they accumulated prior to their retirements. Finally, we meet three people who demonstrate that working part-time in retirement can substantially improve the retirement experience.

Tip Anderson – *An Innocent Mistake*

TIP ANDERSON'S* FAMILY moved from Cleveland to the outskirts of Atlanta when he was in the fifth grade. He had a difficult childhood. Tip and his two sisters were abused by his father, and in the late 1930s and early 1940s it was a challenge to grow up in the rural South with a Northern accent. Tip escaped by reading, and he came to love the solitude of the library. He received his undergraduate and law degrees from the University of Virginia and went into antitrust litigation with the Department of Justice in the 1950s. Tip later became a prominent attorney with a large Chicago law firm where he litigated securities, contract, antitrust, and patent cases. He remarried after his first marriage ended in divorce. With the merging of two families, he and his second wife, Marsha, had seven kids.

While he had enjoyed law school and practicing law, by his mid-fifties Tip started looking for new work. "But once I became an established litigator, there was no way for me to get out of it. I didn't have clients of my own. I'd handle a case, and when it

* pseudonym

was over I'd never see the client again. The only thing that changed in my life was that the decimal kept moving farther and farther to the right. I started out with $1,500 cases, then $15,000 cases, then $150,000 cases, then $1,500,000, and then $15,000,000. The pressure kept increasing—involving more and more people, and taking more and more time. It got to me—the pressure to win and the pressure to please the clients. I knew I needed to get out of litigation. I wanted to find an in-house counsel position. I tried for four or five years during my fifties to find the right situation, but I could never make it 'click.' Then I started looking for a business to buy. After all seven kids were out of high school, the time was right. We didn't have anybody at home anymore, and I didn't want to continue what I was doing."

In 1986, Tip relocated to Tampa, where he bought a small plastic molding company. With no first-hand knowledge of manufacturing the transition was difficult, but his tenacity paid off. Over the next ten years, the business more than tripled in size. With Marsha's encouragement, Tip sold the company on his seventieth birthday and entered the world of retirement financially sound. Though he was somewhat uncertain about what to do next, his transition into retirement went smoothly. Over the next two years, he spent a lot of time sailing and playing golf and tennis. Little did he know that his biggest problems were yet to come.

The sale of the business turned out to be a nightmare. "I had borrowed a lot of money to buy presses and other equipment to grow the business. You can't run a small company without guaranteeing all of the notes at the bank. Then the buyer failed, and I ended up having to take the company back. I finally found another buyer and got out of it by selling the equipment to him. But I ended up with a huge debt to the bank. I lost more than a million dollars on the deal. I had to sell my yacht club and golf club memberships to get cash. I have had financial problems ever since. It changed my life."

Fortunately, Tip and Marsha had always kept their finances separate. "Since it's a second marriage for both of us, we have a pre-nuptial agreement. We run the household fifty-fifty. But I would not be able to afford the house I live in if it weren't for aggressive refinancing. I am even using Marsha's credit with Merrill Lynch." Tip has some real estate investments, and he devotes a tremendous amount of effort making them generate cash to pay down his bank obligations. "I have to spend a lot of time figuring out how to improve the investments, negotiating things, dealing with tenants, and appealing the tax assessments.

"I may have been retired for a while, but I'm not now. I spend my time trying to salvage my life from the bad sale of a good company. But if you're fighting a battle, the pain is not the point. The battle is the point. All of my legal experience has helped me get through this so far, but it's not over. I don't know if it ever will be."

Now in his late seventies, Tip is not finding much joy in life. "I'm not very happy now, probably because when I look into the future I don't see anything to be enthusiastic about. I don't have many personal friends, and I am not much of a community person. My relationship with my wife is a bit strained because I can't afford to travel as much as she wants to. I spend so much of my time on minutia and errands and trying to figure out how to work my way out of the problems I've got. Fighting off the demons of failure has been depressing. Bills are coming in and going out, and keeping it all in balance is a challenge. I don't recommend it. We maintain our home, but that's only because Marsha is financially set. So she's able to carry the things that I simply can't."

Tip's story emphasizes the importance of having financial security during retirement. Michael Stein and Mike Sargent, two of the country's leading financial planners, explain what people should do to ensure a happier outcome.

Michael Stein –
Rethinking Retirement Planning

MICHAEL STEIN'S PATH to becoming one of the more insightful financial planners in the country was unconventional. He went to West Point and became an Army officer. Later, he graduated with honors from American University with a specialization in Soviet studies. He was assigned to Garmisch-Partenkirchen, Germany, for additional post-graduate work and then was transferred to Berlin and given intelligence-gathering responsibilities.

"When I went to Berlin, the Russians were starting to install a ground-to-air missile system around the city to increase their ability to hamper another Berlin airlift. I picked up on it early when I saw a network of communications towers being built with parabolic dishes on them. Then I noticed that they were building garages near many of these locations. I went into one of the garages and found that there were no roofs—the garage doors went up the side and over the top. This told us where they were going to put their missiles. We also discovered buried telephone cables between these installations, and I managed to find a telephone junction box. I put a bug on it that somebody in Washington had built out of East German parts.

"It was pretty clever. If the Russians had found it they would have thought that the East German secret police were spying on them. We were able to listen to all their tests, learn their procedures, and we had the whole thing figured out before they had it in operation. I ended up with the Army's second highest peacetime award for that bit of work."

On another occasion, a Russian sentry shot at Michael and

two of his fellow officers while they were attempting to observe Russian troop maneuvers. He laughed as he recalled, "There is tremendous satisfaction in being shot at and missed. It's really a wonderful feeling!"

In 1977, after twenty years of active duty involving other defense intelligence assignments in Vietnam, Washington, and London, Michael retired from the Army and began his financial planning career. He attacked this new endeavor with the ardor he had demonstrated in the Army, ending up as a regional director for a California broker/dealer with about fifty financial planners working under his direction. By 1995, he was financially secure and had had enough. "Managing financial planners was like herding cats."

"I retired, but when I was cleaning out my desk I discovered that I had a file drawer full of great stuff about problems with the traditional retirement planning model. So I decided to write a book about it, because I felt that I had something important to say that other people weren't talking about. The basic message was that people were planning for the wrong retirements. They were planning for the retirements of their parents' generation, not their own. They weren't considering their increased personal expectations, their longer expected life spans, or the impact of future inflation. Their planning was totally outdated."

Don Phillips, president and CEO of Morningstar, called Michael's book, *The Prosperous Retirement*, "required reading . . . a how-to guide for reinventing retirement." In the book, Michael addresses the risks of retirement and the common shortcomings he sees in the traditional retirement planning process. "People face a whole series of financial risks, and as far as I'm concerned the only solution for that is a two-phase program of diversification and management. You have to have a diversified investment portfolio, and you have to pay attention to your budget and your assets and the relationship between your budget and your assets.

You have to pay attention to changes in tax and estate planning laws, and if you don't want to do that you have to hire professionals to do it for you. If you don't, you could end up with devastating consequences.

"The first few years of retirement can be the most active and enjoyable period of a person's life—like a second childhood without parental supervision. Once they are freed from having to go to work every day, many people find great joy in pursuing their athletic, philanthropic, intellectual, spiritual, and avocational interests. They will probably travel more, and that is not inexpensive. So my first observation about retirement is that the active-phase retirement budget tends to equal the pre-retirement budget—if the retiree can afford it.

"One of the challenges in retirement is to not get caught up in a competitive race with your friends. People often want to take trips that are nicer or more exotic than their neighbors' trips, or to buy fancier things. This can get really expensive and that tendency has to be held in check, but it is hard because everyone wants to have the best retirement possible.

"After a while, though, the 'go-go' phase of retirement gives way to the 'slow-go' phase. Older people take fewer trips and then, ultimately, no trips. They buy no new cars, no new houses, and fewer new clothes. They may downsize. So they evolve into a quieter and less expensive lifestyle. Their annual expenses may actually decline by twenty-five percent or more, although some of that decline can be offset by inflation.

"It is not necessary to have a huge amount of money to have a good retirement. It is just as possible to have a happy retirement on a limited budget as it is to have a happy pre-retirement life on a limited budget. But it is hard to imagine a happy retirement when you are constantly dogged by worries about finances."

One of the keys is to be realistic. "My clients almost always had pessimistic expectations about their longevity. They didn't expect to live as long as they probably were going to live. That colored their investment decisions and how they lived their lives and how they spent their money. Many of my clients were unwilling to think about it. But that wasn't really surprising, because a lot people never gave *any* consideration to retirement until late in their working lives.

"Many of my clients assumed that they were going to die in their own homes and in their own beds. And a lot of them thought that they had the option of moving in with their kids in their later years. I had to force them to look at those assumptions and consider the alternatives. I would ask them, 'Is that the memory that you want to leave with your family? The picture of an old man cloistered in the basement? If you don't have any other options that may be something you will have to do. But think through the alternatives before that becomes your only option.'"

Having sufficient money means having more options, but it is only one step toward a satisfying retirement. "Many people who have devoted their lives to the single-minded goal of becoming wealthy may not have developed the other skills that will be required to make retirement a success. So while some people have to focus their pre-retirement planning on wealth accumulation, there are others whose pre-retirement planning should focus on developing the interests and skills that will be necessary for a good retirement — namely physical and mental health, diet and exercise, personal relationships, intellectual stimulation, and spiritual balance. Just because a retiree has lots of money doesn't mean that retirement is going to be all cake and ale.

"In fact, in today's world where retirements can last for thirty or forty years, many people are finding it useful financially, intellectually, and personally to have some sort of post-retirement employment. That can ease the transition from work to leisure and can provide social and intellectual interactions that help keep them involved. Retirement jobs may or may not involve the same kind of work people were previously doing. But typically these jobs have reduced hours, less pressure, and flexible deadlines that make them more compatible with retirement."

Frequently, retirees who are not gainfully employed become active volunteers, but there are no guarantees that volunteer work will be fulfilling. Many people agree with Michael, who found that serving as a director of non-profit boards was not the solution for him. "It is really hard to find a satisfying volunteer position. Volunteer organizations are usually run by zealous people who may be unwilling to let other people invade their little fiefdoms. They want to be the kings or queens. If you become involved and make any sounds like you have management aspirations, you become a threat, and they will find ways of marginalizing you. The one place that you are absolutely welcome in any volunteer organization is as a fundraiser, but most people are not really excited about becoming fundraisers. I know I am not."

At this point, Michael's volunteer activities are limited to hands-on activities rather than directorships. "Now I'm a grandparent, a tutor for disadvantaged kids, a historical preservationist, a woodworker, and a bunch of other small things that I'll continue with as long as they are fun. I love to read, I love to follow politics, and I enjoy carving. I am finding that this is just a wonderful stage of my life."

Michael sees retirement as a time during which we should use our life's learning to capitalize on opportunities we find interesting. "Retirement is not automatically a great time in life, even for people for whom life has been wonderful. We must manage the changes, have appropriate expectations, and focus our energies on things that will scratch where we itch. Not everyone needs relevance; some people will gladly settle for tranquility and inner peace. Some can draw on past achievements, while others need to keep climbing mountains. It's up to each individual to set his or her own course, and both financial and non-financial considerations are part of that."

Mike Sargent –
What Farmers Know That Others Don't

MIKE SARGENT IS AN ANOMALY: he's an effervescent CPA. When he enters the room, the energy level explodes with his enthusiasm. His early career was marked by success in Arthur Young & Company's tax department, after which he became a chief financial and investment officer for a wealthy individual who had diverse investment interests. Mike then became a Certified Financial Planner and started his own investment career. He took his family to Australia for a five-month escape before founding Sargent & Company (now Sargent Bickham & Associates), a leading financial advisory firm. *Worth* magazine named Mike one of the one hundred top financial advisors in the U.S., and Charles Schwab & Company selected him from their pool of more than 5,000 independent advisors to serve on their financial advisor board. He knows what he's doing.

Mike's advisory firm adopted an eclectic approach. "My business was different from that of most money managers because we offered a broader range of services. We provided financial consulting, problem solving, tax planning, stock option strategies, and estate planning. We helped set up employee benefit plans. We invested in real estate deals as well as in marketable securities. So, we really were the focal point for many clients' financial planning."

One of his retirement planning tools was truly unique. "I would prepare a non-financial balance sheet that identified my clients' non-financial assets, such as abilities, talents, education, potential inheritance, working spouse, good health, and the energy and ability to go back to work. It also included their liabilities, such as poor health, family obligations, or poor spending habits. This exercise would help them address some of the personal and emotional issues they needed to consider along with the financial issues in retirement planning." This proved to be invaluable for the dozens of people he advised as they approached retirement.

By the time Mike started his own retirement, the pressure of managing other people's retirement funds had taken its toll. "I felt that in my business I had as close a relationship with my clients as their doctors and ministers did. And the stress was just huge. I couldn't sleep if the market was down. I took every loss in every client account worse than I took it in my own account. They all had told me that they were relying on me. In other words, they transferred their 'money-stress' to me. So I would worry about their retirements. If something went wrong, I would call while I was on my vacation. On vacation I would constantly be making notes to myself about how to improve our performance. I took a note pad and pen with me even when I went on a walk to make sure any ideas that came to me would not get away. It just never stopped. I could not relax. After I retired it was a whole new ballgame. Getting rid of that stress was just awesome. Now I can go on a walk and just enjoy it. Life is a hundred times better."

Mike discussed the financial risks that retirees face. "The biggest risks are improper planning and the failure to take action when a plan is in place. Remember how you used to cram for finals when you were in college? Well, preparing for retirement is not like cramming for a college final. It's more like farming. You don't see a farmer cramming his work into one week. He has to plant his crops and fertilize them and water them and let them grow before he thinks about harvesting. It's important to start as early as you can. The people with the most security in retirement have taken the farmer's approach, not the college student's.

"The financial risks of retirement differ with each client. But one common risk is unrealistic expectations, thinking that the market will do better over the long run than it actually does. This may be less of a problem now, after the market bust in 2000, but there are still people who believe that the rapid growth rates seen in the 1990s will come back. That's a bad bet.

"Closely related to that is retiring without what Warren Buffett calls a 'margin of safety'—thinking that nothing bad will happen when, in fact, it is almost certain that something bad *will* happen. It's important to have a good cushion. You usually can come pretty close to projecting your financial needs if you use reasonable assumptions about your spending, inflation, how long you're going to live, projected rates of return, and other factors. There are several places you can go that will help with this analysis. The web sites at Quicken, mutual funds such as T. Rowe Price, and Charles Schwab are good resources. But you can never know about all the unexpected events that might disrupt your financial plans. For example, what happens if one of your kids gets a divorce or becomes ill when they don't have health insurance? It is important to have a big financial margin of safety before you feel comfortable that you have enough.

"Another problem is being either too aggressive or too conservative with your investment portfolio. You have to manage risk, but you can't become so conservative that you are not properly protected against inflation. Diversification of investments is very important, and failure to diversify is one of the biggest reasons people have gotten in trouble. Another big risk is debt. In retirement you don't want to have as much debt as you had when you were earning a regular salary. Obviously, being debt-free is best.

"A lot of young people make the mistake of not living within their means, believing that their financial situation will improve as they get older and make more money. But these same people keep increasing their expenses, and they never do get ahead. The hard truth is that cutting expenses is the surest way to reach your goals. That is the message in the book *The Millionaire Next Door*.

"Even in later years, one of the most common problems is that one or the other spouse does not keep spending under control. Bad habits do not change when you inherit money or retire. Having money merely exaggerates who a person already is. If you have a bad financial habit, it will continue and maybe even get worse. You can get in trouble early on if you spend more money than is coming in.

"People in retirement have a lot more idle time, and often that is filled by spending money. They do things they didn't do earlier in their lives because now they have the time. It's easy to let that get out of hand. Some clients have taken retirement funds that were a key source of their income and converted them to non-productive assets, like remodeling their homes or buying vacation homes. It's important to distinguish between personal assets that are used for living and investment assets that are the sources of income you will need.

"One key issue is who handles the money. Often only one of the two people in a marriage controls the finances, and when that person dies the spouse may not have the skills necessary to manage properly. So, making sure that both spouses are financially competent is really important. One good way to do that is for both people to be involved in all of the couple's financial decisions.

"Another risk is divorce, which is becoming more common among people in their fifties and sixties — after the kids have grown. All of a sudden the assets are split and they have two households and all of the other additional expenses. When that happens, the retirement funds they had thought would be adequate may not be.

"A hidden risk is your kids' health insurance. You'd better make sure that they have it because if they don't and something happens, you will end up paying for it. And your kids can be unexpected financial burdens in other ways. One problem that many people have had is being overly generous with gifts and financial aid to children and grandchildren."

One issue that occurs too frequently is inadequate retirement savings. "It's a real dilemma. You can take on extra risk to try to catch up, but if your investment strategy fails, you end up in worse shape, and then you have even less time to catch up. So that probably is not the right way to go. You have to be realistic, and that means you either have to work longer, you have to cut your living expenses so that you can get your savings back on track, or you can shorten your life expectancy by smoking and riding motorcycles. Those are your choices. You may not like them, but that's reality."

Many people work during retirement, but their motivations differ. "There are two reasons people go back to work, and they are totally different. Some people are forced to go back for financial reasons, and others go for social reasons or to increase their sense of self-worth or just to get some mental stimulation. You surely don't want to be forced to go back to work. Technology is changing daily, and your skill set may have become outdated. You might not be able to get a job. Also, whether we like it or not, age discrimination is a reality—especially in the well-paying jobs."

As important as financial planning is, Mike believes that more attention should be directed to non-financial planning. "Most of the focus has been on estate planning, on setting up trusts and saving taxes and making sure your assets go to your kids. But what has not been as fully addressed is the idea of getting those assets into the hands of kids who have the right values and have the common sense to manage their lives properly. I've handled many clients who have inherited money, and I have seen the horrible decisions that they make, the total waste of the financial capital that may have taken their parents a lifetime to build. So a big question is: How do you transfer your non-financial assets—your values and common sense? The point is that you first have to make sure that you have given your kids the management tools before they get the money. They should have the ability to make good financial decisions, and they should have value systems that you respect. Both of these are important, because kids can be good decision makers with bad values or lousy decision makers with great values. Kids need both skill sets. To be good parents, you have to be involved with them and help them to learn how to do things the right way.

"This is not something that is over when the kids leave the house. We still involve our kids annually in our charitable gift decisions. We have also offered to pay for certain classes that we thought would be helpful in their personal growth. We paid for all three of our kids to go to Dale Carnegie training because we thought it could make a difference in their lives. I may even pay for golf school because I think a good golf game can be a valuable business asset for them to have."

Now in retirement, Mike focuses tremendous energy on helping his family prosper in all respects. "You spend the first half of your life seeking success and should spend the second half seeking significance. I have devoted an incredible amount of time to my kids and my brother and sisters. I spend a lot of time strategizing with the kids. It's a gift that I would never have been able to give before—because I didn't have the time. And we have gotten much closer; I've become their secret weapon. They can be working on something and they know that they can call and

ask Dad if they want help. This has given me a great deal of joy, but I have to admit that my stress now seems to come from worrying about all of my family members."

While Michael Stein and Mike Sargent planned their own retirements well and are thriving now that they have left their careers behind them, probably more than half of future retirees will work part-time during at least a portion of their retirement years. In fact, according to *AARP Bulletin*, an AARP survey of working people between the ages of forty-five and seventy-four found that seven out of ten respondents would work during their retirement years. Many of them concluded that they would do so "even if they were financially set for life."

Juanee Mitchell – *Why Yoda Works*

JUANEE MITCHELL'S RURAL ILLINOIS SCHOOL had twelve students in its eight grades, and her mother was her teacher for six of the eight years. Not surprisingly, she gravitated toward education and became a high school teacher and then a college instructor. By 1979, however, she was ready for a change and recognized the emerging opportunities in the computer science field. She took a two-year course in computer programming and went to work for the National Center of Atmospheric Research (NCAR), where she worked full-time until 1997.

"I went to work for the Scientific Computing Division at NCAR. That is the division that furnishes the computing power so that all of the solar physicists, atmospheric scientists, and oceanographers can run their models. We used to have the most powerful computers in the world, but now everything is done with hundreds of networked PCs.

"I started out as a technician. Then I took more computer courses and became a programmer. That later evolved into managing the database, tracking users, and monitoring their budgets. When I was full-time, many of my duties were routine, but it was stressful. There was a lot of pressure. Whenever my group made a mistake, the computers were shut down and nobody could work. And those machines ran twenty-four hours a day, seven days a week.

"In 1997, I was planning to retire cold turkey, but they asked me if I would work on an hourly basis, and I agreed. So I retired and there was a big party. And the day after I retired I went off to New Zealand for a month. While I was gone, they called me to ask if I would work on a special project as soon as I got home. I did, and I have been working a flexible schedule since then. It has really made my retirement much better than it would have been. In fact, the most interesting work that I have done has been since I retired and went back on a part-time basis.

"At first I didn't work many hours, but gradually that changed. Finally they said, 'Well, you can work as much as you want.' Now I am working half-time, and under federal law they had to put me back on the payroll, with employee and retirement benefits. One of the reasons they called me back was that they were shorthanded, but another part was that I had the background and experience. No one is irreplaceable, and I tried to train people and document everything. But I guess it was just easier for them to call me, so they did. My co-workers nicknamed me Yoda and put his picture on my office door.

"When I work now, I still feel pressure, but not as much as before. I don't take the problems home with me very often, and I can take time off because I'm on my own schedule. That helps a lot. Plus, I really like the people; I wouldn't work there if I didn't. And I like the job because now I am doing interesting things like problem solving and figuring out new programs and procedures. It's like doing puzzles: You have a beginning and an end. I keep learning new things, and I love the challenge. But at NCAR I don't have to do it all alone. NCAR has always been on the cutting edge, and I have all these experts that I can talk to and tap into their knowledge.

"I also enjoy working now because it gives me a sense of feeling productive, and I like the structure that it gives to my life. Otherwise, I feel a little aimless. I usually go to work early, and if I don't go to work I end up sitting around reading the paper. I don't seem to get much done. Working also gives me a challenge I wouldn't otherwise have in my life. And I like getting paid for it. It allows me to do a lot of things that I would not be able to do otherwise. I'm very happy in my little niche.

"Coming from a thrifty and busy family that worked from dawn to dusk, I always felt that working was expected. But even though work has always been a big part of my life, I have never let it consume me. My working friends are not a large part of my social life. I've always had my tennis friends, my teaching friends, neighbors, and other groups.

"In fact, I think retirement is often easier for women than it is for men — even when a spouse dies. Women usually have circles of friends and activities that aren't dependent on their husbands. But some men are lost when their wives die because they are so dependent. By the way, that's one of the advantages of small towns. The neighbors are closer and much more willing to help each other out.

"I haven't had any problems in retirement. Fortunately, I've had my health, but that is always a concern. At some point, I won't, and so I don't want to put off doing things that I might not be able to do later.

"When I retired I wasn't going to have a tremendous amount of income, but I figured that I could live comfortably on what I would have. Now because of my job I have a lot more money to do with as I choose. I live better, I travel more, and I can do more things for my kids. I've taken them on some of my trips. New Zealand was a great trip, and I've been to Churchill, Canada, to see the polar bears, the Galapagos Islands, on an Alaskan cruise, and to Costa Rica. Probably the best trip was to Machu Picchu, Peru, to the lost city of the Incas. It's off the beaten path and there aren't many tourists. I'm still planning to go to Nepal, China, Australia, and Chile.

"Most of the trips have been with some kind of group. I've gone with Elderhostel and Grand Circle, and an offshoot of that called Overseas Adventure Tours. Elderhostel used to be really spartan, but they have upgraded because they realized that people wanted more than just college dorms and dorm food. You can still find good values, and some of trips are really active with hiking, bicycling, touring, and cruising. I usually go with a friend, but many people go alone."

Even though she works half-time, Juanee has wanted to volunteer somewhere, but it hasn't worked out. "I have looked around at volunteering, and it's really competitive to get the interesting positions. It seems like the only things available are low level, with somebody always telling you what to do. I'm not used to being on the bottom rung; I'm used to calling my own shots. At NCAR I am able to use the skills that I developed during my career. That is not very often the case in volunteer positions."

Juanee's frustration with finding rewarding volunteer positions reconfirms what several other people said. But Barb Page came to a different conclusion. In fact, she turned a part-time volunteer position into a full-time paying job.

Barb Page – *When Volunteering Pays*

BARB PAGE GREW UP IN THE TEXAS PANHANDLE and graduated from the University of Oklahoma. Her husband, Bob, became an aerospace engineer, and Barb became what she calls a country club wife — a Junior Leaguer, PTA mom, and housewife.

But her life would change. In 1974, Bob decided he wanted a new challenge, and he and a partner bought a small meat canning company. Five years later, Bob and Barb bought the partner out and Barb went to work full-time. From 1979 to 1998, when they sold the company, annual sales increased from $1 million to $17 million. But it was not a smooth ride.

"Bob was president and was responsible for all operations. I was CFO and oversaw the administrative and financial areas. It was very much a family business. During one five year period we had the two of us, three sons, one daughter-in-law, an ex-daughter-in-law and a fiancé all on the payroll, along with 110 other employees. It was unbelievable. I would not recommend it to anyone who wants to remain married or sane, though it worked out well in the end. We have great memories and wonderful stories, but I am not sure that we would be willing to do it over again.

"I hope I am not being chauvinistic when I say this, but I think that women are pretty good managers of their lives and pretty good at juggling a lot of things at one time. A big part of that is because of what we go through and learn in rearing children and managing our homes. I know good and well that is why I was able to go into a small company and grow with it. I knew how to juggle, and without any other training I don't think I could have done that if I hadn't been a mom first.

"Looking back at working together, first as a couple and then as a family, there are many more happy and good memories than sad or bad ones. We all watched each other grow. We laughed a lot. We know we did a lot of good for our employees. We made some fabulous friends in the industry. We were survivors. And finally, we created a success story. There is a lot to be said for all of that!

"When we sold, we all had three-year employment agreements with the buyer. But the buyer ended up having to make some personnel cutbacks. Even though he was technically obligated to me, I didn't want to work anymore. So I got out of there, and I had about nine months of full-time retirement. It was enough time to really whet my appetite for retirement; I can tell you that much!"

Barb's well-earned retirement was interrupted by a new challenge: Craig Hospital. Craig is a world-renowned center for spinal cord injury and brain injury rehabilitation. Most of its patients have suffered tragic accidents that confine them to wheelchairs for the rest of their lives. "I had been on the board at Craig Hospital for more than four years, but because I had been so busy, I had never had the time to make a major contribution. We had talked about starting a capital campaign to solve some of the hospital's physical needs and adapt to the changes taking place in the health care industry. I agreed to help out about a half day a week, but that grew into a five day a week full-time volunteer job. I did that for a year and a half. During that time, we got a half million dollar Kresge grant and decided that we should hire a full-time director of development. Then they asked me if I would take the job.

"At first, I didn't want to work full-time, because we had been planning to spend every other month in our vacation townhouse in Dana Point, California. But you can't spend any time at Craig and not be committed to the hospital. I love the patients, I love the staff, I love the mission, and I love the management. So that is where I need to be right now. The other thing is that the stock market didn't cooperate the way that we thought it should, and it's helpful for me to work for a while longer. Plus, I am not sixty-five yet and I get full medical coverage from Craig. So, for a lot of reasons it makes sense to stay involved.

"I never thought I would go into fundraising. No way! But fundraising is people, and I love people. And I am learning. And we have had success. We raised seven million dollars in eighteen months in a weak economy. That feels great. To be honest, I don't take a lot of the credit for that because we have such a fabulous president who commands incredible respect in the community.

"The other benefit of being here is that I think it keeps me younger—mentally, physically, and emotionally. I know it keeps me happy. I may have a million things on my mind. But when I look around and see what the patients have to deal with, I think, 'I don't have one thing to bitch about. Life is good!' Plus, it's always a joy having other people count on you. We all like to have our egos boosted. It's an interesting scenario because not only do I feel the joy of being needed, I feel the pressure of being needed.

"I have always had a real strong belief in God. A lot of people in here might say, 'How can you believe in God when you see the kind of horrendous accidents that have happened and when you see the injuries these people have to live with?' Well, God didn't cause that. And I believe that your faith is going to bring you through life's challenges and help you to be a better person.

"We bought long-term care insurance before I started working at Craig. But I can guarantee you that if we had not had it when I started working here, we would have had it within two weeks. All you have to do is see that many of the patients who leave here will still need full-time care. Who can afford that? Most people can't, and so it falls on their families. The toll it takes on those families is enormous. It's brutal! What is interesting is that the people I know who have a lot of money do not have long-term care insurance because they say they don't need it. But wait. If you have enough money, what difference does that $6,000 per year make? And then, no matter what happens you are covered and your kids won't ever have to think about it."

Barb expects to continue to work at Craig for another two or three years, and she believes that some of the current pressures will be reduced. "If I can get this thing going in the direction I want, I won't feel frantic when I am not here. Now I mentally take the job home with me all the time. Even when we travel, I take my laptop and I call in and am online every day."

Barb's dedication is well known among her friends. "People who have known me for a long time say, 'Ha ha. See! I told you that you could never retire. You will never be able to not work.' And that's because I am such a high-energy person. And yet, I'm pretty happy on the back deck of our vacation home. I am very content walking on the beach, reading, and enjoying nature. But I also love to be active. So if I had two cents worth of advice to people, I would say that the old adage about having interests other than your work—and getting a balance to your life—is absolutely true.

"It's going to be harder to leave Craig than it was to leave our own company because of the people and the mission. Whether I really am contributing or not, who knows? But I feel like I am, and that is what brings me in here every day with a smile on my face. And the extra money and the health insurance are great also. The extra money means enough to me that if someone said I could do it in four or eight hours a week, just enough to give me some mad money, I would do it in a heartbeat. To me there is a big difference between retiring with a gazillion dollars and retiring with what is going to keep me comfortable. Sure, we can live comfortably. But can we live exactly the way we want to for the rest of our days? Maybe not. So the extra money makes a difference. For me there is a huge value to that."

Still, Barb looks forward to the days when she can make her own schedule. "I would love to study photography and take classes at the Botanic Gardens. I love the outdoors and hiking and watching birds. I want to do as much outdoors while I still have my health. I also want to spend more time at home. I love the computer. We have five grandkids, and the time we spend with them is great. I look forward to being fully retired someday. But I also believe in what I am doing at Craig. I love the people contact, and I am learning so much. So I think I'll be here for a while longer.

"I think I'll always feel that I can make a difference with my family in general and my grandchildren in particular. And I hope I'll be able to make some financial contributions. Beyond that I don't know that I'll have to do much more. Frankly, I hope I don't feel that need." She deserves that freedom.

Lee Woodward – *Redefining Retirement*

AFTER GRADUATING FROM LAW SCHOOL and serving as a Navy JAG Corps officer near Tokyo, Lee Woodward returned to Indiana to practice law. After a while his hometown seemed too small, and Lee concluded, "I was fat, dumb, and not all that happy." He moved to Phoenix and joined an agricultural real estate firm, ultimately heading up their real estate brokerage operations. With over $1 billion in properties for sale, Lee concluded that they needed to streamline the real estate valuation process, and in 1982 he bought a personal computer (PC) to help implement his plan. In time, he and the company parted ways because of differing viewpoints, and this led to one of his most important insights.

"The best things I got out of that whole experience were that little PC and the understanding that people were going to adopt the new technology. I wanted to take advantage of that, but I figured that I didn't know anything about manufacturing computers and I didn't know anything about selling them. The opportunity for me was in financing them, so I went into the leasing business. The company, Computer Access, didn't work out very well for the first few years. We over-expanded and ran out of money, the usual things that start-ups do. I knew I could figure it out, and I knew I could be successful. But I also knew I had to grow and change if I was going to make it work. The main business turned out to be thirty- to ninety-day rentals. Our real growth came later when we started selling equipment and became an authorized dealer for Compac, HP, IBM, Apple, Toshiba—the whole range. We went from five million to over a hundred million dollars in sales."

Lee's management philosophy was one of the reasons his company was successful. "I had a mantra and I gave this speech repeatedly: 'Our business will be driven by three things. We are going to take very good care of our customers. No business is successful unless it does that. We are going to grow the business, because the only way to create opportunities for everybody in this room is to grow. And finally, we are going to have fun doing it, because we all are going to be a lot happier if we wake up in the morning and look forward to going to work.' Not everybody bought into that mantra, but most people did. And I can't tell you how many former Computer Access people have told me that it was the best place they ever worked. That was my goal. But you go to the big companies and having fun isn't even on their list of things to do. Large corporations are just a different world.

"By 1996 the hardware sales were generating about eighty percent of our revenues, and people were knocking on the door wanting to buy our business. Since competition was increasing and our margins were falling, we agreed to sell.

"I didn't want to retire in the traditional sense. But I had worked an average of between eighty-five and ninety hours a week for fifteen years, and I didn't want to go back to that either. For one thing, I wasn't sure I had the physical stamina to do that anymore. So my goal has been to work about forty weeks a year. We have a house in British Columbia and I would like to spend some time there. My parents are in their eighties and still live on their farm. I have family responsibilities there that need more time and attention. So I have been looking for a part-time executive position.

"After I sold the business, I was a director in two or three little companies, but that didn't work because of who I am. I always want to get involved in the operations to correct the mistakes that I see management making. I want to have hands-on responsibility. But they don't want to hear about it; they want to do things their way. So it hasn't worked out.

"After I sold in 1997, I came to the conclusion that the stock market was overvalued. I was wrong about the timing, but in the long run was right about the value. We were just paying too dearly for future earnings. I decided I would rather build an office building than be in the stock market. So we built a new building right next to the one we had kept when we sold the business. The new building is fully leased and everything there is pretty solid. But the tenant who took over the old building wanted to convert it into a big data center. They had $830 million in the bank, which sounded great. But they were trying to build out more than forty data centers around the country, and it didn't work. They ended up filing for bankruptcy, and I took a big hit as well.

"We haven't gone hungry, and we still have a nice place to live. But we have definitely had some financial stress since they filed for bankruptcy. At least there was *some* good news. Because of a provision I had put in the lease, I ended up with all of the equipment that had been delivered to our building. So I decided to go into the data center business myself. I need to get this on track. It's similar to what I have done before, and I think the company is headed on the right course.

"Still, my goals on the financial side are pretty modest. I have sought financial independence, but I never sought to make a huge amount of money. What drives me is to have fun growing businesses and to have a bit more time to myself. And I think I may be able to accomplish that with this business. I have a partner and co-worker who I can do some job-sharing with, and we get along great.

"I expect to stay active in the business world indefinitely. My goal is to scale down my level of activity but not to make it go away. My business life is a big part of how I view myself. I think I have something to contribute. I've been able to spur job growth. I've been able to send lots of people to college. I'm very proud of that, and I want to continue doing it. I have received tremendous rewards from the business community, and I'm not talking about the financial rewards. It's the people, it's the challenge, and it's the pride that comes with building successful businesses. I have no interest in retirement in the traditional sense, where life just comes to a screeching halt. I just don't see it. I can only work out so much.

"I haven't given up the idea that I can be a benefit to companies as a board member. I just haven't executed that plan very well. So I am going to actively seek out opportunities where I can make a contribution. I am very interested in that. I have tried working with non-profits, and I may give that another shot.

"I think that the people who enjoy what they do and find ways to scale back their workloads are happier than the people who retire from jobs that they didn't like. I remember as a kid, seeing one farmer who retired and sat in a rocking chair. He was dead in about six months. Meanwhile another 'curmudgeonly' old farmer was out working in his fields at eighty-four. It just always occurred to me that I would rather be the latter instead of the former. Sitting in a rocking chair just doesn't work. You just can't get that rocker to go fast enough!"

Observations about Preparing Financially

THE PEOPLE INTERVIEWED FOR THIS CHAPTER confirm that each of us must find happiness and fulfillment in our own way. Michael Stein was correct when he said that some people need mountains to climb, while others are content with tranquility and inner peace. Many of us want to work during at least a few of our retirement years, but others abhor the thought of it. Clearly, retirement does not necessarily mean not working. Rather, it means having the flexibility to live our lives as we wish. *Retirement is the culmination of our lifelong drive toward the freedom of our choosing.*

Tip Anderson's story shows that freedom cannot exist when we are burdened with financial obligations beyond our means. Money is a source of stress, and the stress is most pronounced for people who do not have enough. To avoid this fate, we should:

- Start planning and saving early

- Be responsible and realistic

- Match our lifestyles to our resources

- Assess our strengths and weaknesses

- Identify potential risks

- Get competent financial advice if we are unsure of how to manage our financial affairs

- Separate investment and personal assets

- Adopt an investment strategy that is neither too conservative nor too aggressive

- Make sure we have the proper insurance

- Invest wisely by diversifying investment assets

margin of safety

- Ensure that our sources of retirement income are reliable

- Move toward eliminating debt

- Budget with special sensitivity to taxes and insurance

- Set aside funds for emergencies

- If in a relationship, make sure that both partners are financially literate

The extent to which we succeed in doing these things will determine how much we are able to reduce financial stress. Nevertheless, despite all of our planning, we should expect financial surprises to occur. They do for almost everybody, and they come when least expected. Disability. Pension fund failures. Children or grandchildren in need. Disease. That is why creating a margin of safety is so important.

But what happens when that margin of safety is not large enough? We must adapt. It won't be easy, but it probably won't be nearly as devastating as we imagined. At this stage of life, material belongings are not as critical as we once thought them to be. The kids have moved on, and we don't need the space that was once important. Paradoxically, downsizing may bring greater happiness because it reduces financial stress.

We have found that being adaptable, positive, and involved are critical skills for coping with the problems we face in retirement. Adaptability is particularly important in helping us match our lifestyles to our financial resources. Being positive does not mean being irresponsibly euphoric. A positive attitude must be tempered with realism, because investment markets fluctuate and are subject to precipitous declines without warning. People with financial discipline always have more options than those without discipline because they deal from a position of relative strength.

Our happiness will be dependent, in part, upon our ability to build investment portfolios that offset any shortfalls we will experience from social security and pension funds. We should not retire before we are financially prepared to do so. But if we have accomplished that goal, we should consider retirement when work becomes a habit instead of a pleasure.

For many people, however, working during retirement substantially improves the retirement experience. The increased income and employee benefits provide greater financial security. Additionally, working may bring other lifestyle benefits, including a greater sense of purpose, the satisfaction of feeling productive, daily focus and structure, interactions with people, the joy of feeling needed, personal challenges and growth, a more youthful perspective, and a sense of pride and accomplishment. With such a panoply of benefits, it is not surprising that many people choose to work part-time during the active phase of their retirement.

In any case, we should follow the example of Mike Sargent's conscientious farmer and avoid the approach of the impetuous college student. A combination of long-term planning, discipline, and proper execution will bring about the financial security that helps us overcome the first of the five retirement challenges. Financial security will simplify our lives, and it is also a bellwether for the other four retirement challenges. A poor financial condition or poor spending habits can adversely affect our ability to adapt to retirement, our health, our relationships with others, and our sense of self-esteem. This is just one reason why it is so important to properly address this first challenge.

FOUR

THE SECOND CHALLENGE:
Making the Transition

(What does it take to successfully shift gears?)

BEING FINANCIALLY PREPARED is an important step, but it provides no assurance that there will be a smooth transition from an intense working life to a more unstructured retirement life. We all go through a period of adjustment as we withdraw from roles that helped define us and move on to new activities. Making a successful transition is our second challenge. For many, this transition is relatively untroubled; for others, it is painfully difficult. In either case, the importance of a successful transition cannot be overstated. Failure to make the appropriate adjustments can result in stress, financial difficulties, health problems, family relationship issues, and doubts about self-esteem.

Transitional problems are compounded for couples. Entering retirement, they must reexamine the way they will live together by addressing personal expectations and responsibilities, changing lifestyles, and the conflicting needs for companionship, independence, sharing, and privacy. Since these social interaction issues transcend the initial adjustment period, they will be addressed in the Chapter Six discussion about relationships.

In this chapter, we will focus on the importance of making personal adjustments. We meet six people who have confronted a variety of transitional challenges. From them, we learn *who* has difficulties adjusting to retirement, *why* they do, and *what* can be done to overcome these challenges.

Dede Bartlett – *Reinventing Yourself*

DEDE BARTLETT IS THE CONSUMMATE PLANNER, organizer, and manager. For her, happiness and fulfillment are found in doing important things well. She exudes commitment, self-confidence, and professionalism.

After graduating from Vassar, Dede worked in public relations during the day, while earning a master's degree in American history at New York University at night. She then joined Mobil Oil, where she held nine positions in fifteen years, including corporate secretary and director of the Mobil Foundation. She moved to Philip Morris as corporate secretary, and later convinced that company to sponsor an initiative to increase worldwide awareness of domestic violence and its tragic implications. This became a high-profile initiative that provided Philip Morris with desperately needed favorable publicity. When it led to numerous action programs to reduce domestic violence around the globe, it also gave Dede a tremendous sense of fulfillment. Her commitment to that cause continues to shape her life.

Like most of us, Dede faced obstacles throughout her career, but for her each represented an opportunity to search within, to analyze who she was and who she wanted to be. "I was lucky because I had some setbacks, and I had to reinvent myself a number of times. In the process, I learned that rather than simply being an employee, I had an entrepreneurial side."

Life in the mainstream of the largest U.S. companies is intense, and balancing multiple roles over time takes its toll. "One of the things that impelled me to take early retirement was that I was burned out physically and emotionally. I really felt that I had to do more with my family and get back in touch with everybody, because I had been overreaching for a long time. I decided I had to get off that train." Her decision came shortly after the terror on September 11, 2001. "My office had a direct view downtown to the towers, and I watched them come down. It was awful. I will never know to what degree that influenced my thinking, but it has to be right up there. It brought home a sense of the fragility of life."

Having made that decision, Dede knew she wanted to create a new life for herself. "I wanted to be moving toward something, not just away from something. I looked at my career and I said, 'This has been a series of adventures, and now it's time to go on to the next one.' I don't look back. I recognized from the beginning that the first year of retirement was going to be a journey. It was the year of the smorgasbord. I wanted to do a number of different things so that I could determine what I might like to concentrate on in the future."

In her first year of retirement, Dede focused on four separate projects. She remained active in supporting efforts to reduce domestic violence, she agreed to take on a foreign-based client who wanted assistance with corporate governance issues, she organized a series of seminars on effective communications in the corporate environment, and she initiated a university-level program on work-life, which addressed the difficult issue for women of achieving balance in their lives. Each of these projects drew upon the skills and interests that Dede had developed during her career.

"I knew that my first year of retirement was going to be a year of self-discovery. I was looking forward to finding out which of the avenues on my smorgasbord I was going to pursue. But, that year my situation turned out to be a lot more complicated than I had expected. We were building a new house. Our daughter got married, and our son had some personal issues that we had to deal with. I had two close colleagues who died, which was very difficult. Plus it brought intimations about mortality. And for all of us, the mortality issue is the elephant in the living room. It's disquieting. So, the year turned into a time of personal adjustment on all of these fronts. Then, on top of everything else, I was involved in the transition to a new lifestyle. There was a lot on my emotional plate!"

Not only did she survive the year, she discovered a new life. "I learned that I adore traveling. I love learning about new places, new cultures, and new foods. I love learning about the history and sociology of new places. I spent my life on the road for Mobil and Philip Morris, traveling overseas for twenty-five years. I loved that. So, I now know that in the quality time remaining I want to take three or four major trips a year and, where possible, combine them with my work and lecturing.

"It is important to me to not just be a travel junky, which can become superficial. So I continue to work on domestic violence issues, and I have four or five venues this year in which I am involved and speaking. The other area is consulting with nonprofit organizations. Because of my background, running the Mobil Foundation for three years and working with several nonprofits groups in the domestic violence area, I have had about thirty groups come to me looking for advice. At first, that was fine, but after a while it became overwhelming. I finally decided to tell them that I would be happy to help for the first couple of hours over lunch or coffee, but beyond that it would have to be on a more formal basis.

"All of this keeps me intellectually alive and growing. That's what I have found is important to achieve the balance that I need. I need the work as the discipline and the intellectual stimulation, and I need the travel as the reward. That will give me the balance that I want."

One project she decided not to pursue was the women's balance issue. "I dropped that because I don't see any solution. I think that the issue of women with careers and children trying to balance their lives is an intractable social problem. And I don't have a happy solution. I see it as only getting worse. The way business is conducted in nanoseconds in the U.S. and around the world, I don't see an easy answer. I don't see employers becoming less rigorous about wanting a 24/7 commitment from their people.

"But for me, retirement was part of the solution to the balance issue that I faced during my career. I was never able to develop hobbies, because working and raising kids and commuting three hours a day didn't leave time for that. I was always in a rush, and I never want to rush again. Rushing is a stress-producer. I rushed to meet the commuter trains. I rushed through my kids' childhoods. I don't want to rush anymore! This past Sunday, our minister talked about everyday miracles, like getting up in the morning. That struck me as being part of the balance we all want, to appreciate what we have and not always be striving for something more. For me, it is terribly important to have an emotional and spiritual balance."

Dede does not look at retirement as an event. She sees it as a process, an evolution. For her, the first year of that process was an exploration of different interests and a search for the activities that would provide the fulfillment she seeks. In subsequent years, her choice of activities may change. But she knows that she is in control and will make changes on her own terms. "When I woke up this morning I said, 'Yes! I worked forty years to be able to wake up at quarter to eight and do what I want to do.'"

Dede's story confirms that despite initial transitional issues, voluntary retirement can lead to the happiness and fulfillment we seek. John Weslar's story shows that involuntary retirement can lead to problems we never foresaw.

John Weslar – *Play the Hand You're Dealt*

JOHN IS ONE OF THE MOST TALENTED PEOPLE I met during my career. After receiving his MBA from Amos Tuck, he worked for General Foods and later for a couple of smaller food processing companies. For twenty-three years, he was single-minded in his devotion to the Coca-Cola Company, serving as a vice president of the Minute Maid division and heading the company's joint venture with Groupe Danon. As he completed his joint-venture assignment in Paris and was returning to the U.S., Coke laid off 7,000 people. Despite his long record of contributions to the company and exemplary reviews throughout his career, John was caught in the tidal wave.

"It's a tough thing to go through. You spend so much of your life working your butt off for a company. You do things that you think are great, and for which you have been recognized and well paid, only to find out that none of that matters. The circumstances change, and no one recognizes your value. It's like that Jack Nicholson movie, *About Schmidt.* The day you walk out of the company, they don't care. They don't appreciate what you did, value what you know, or care about what happens to you. And the crushing thing is that most of the other people in the business world don't care either. You're out there at a complete loss. You know that you're a good person, and you still have a lot to offer, but it doesn't seem to matter to anybody. Your self-esteem goes out the window.

"I never planned for retirement. I had an agreement with Coke that I wasn't even going to consider retiring until I was sixty. And all this happened when I was fifty-seven. If you're a person like me, an 'A' type personality with your whole life based on your work, and suddenly that is taken away, you have to adjust. And that is one hell of an adjustment.

"When I left Coke, they had an outplacement service, and that helped me think through what I was interested in doing. The conclusion I came to is that I wanted to work. I guess I was born to be a workaholic. I just love work. I've never been imbued by a lot of outside interests. I don't play golf or fish. I don't do a lot of things that turn other people on. I've focused my life around my work. Work drives my self-esteem. It drives my income. It drives my network, the whole social structure that I relate to. But after three years, I'm still not employed. With the work gone, I've been experimenting with several different things. I must confess that I have not yet found the solution that will work for me."

His frustration has mounted. "You look for a job, and you think it will be a piece of cake because you have developed some special skills that you know are needed. But it's not easy. You send out your resume. You contact the recruiters. You get on the Internet. You work at building a network. And you run into resistance everywhere. There are age barriers or concerns about how much money you made or questions about whether your background is the right fit. And in almost all cases companies are going to go for someone who is younger, who will work for less, and who they think will be around for another twenty years. After a while, you start spending your time managing your own investments. That keeps you busy, but it doesn't get you where you want to go.

"Now I have more time, but I haven't changed who I am. I wish I could tell you what the right solution is, but I haven't figured it out. I do know that you have to maintain a balance mentally or else you'll be depressed the rest of your life. You have to maintain your self-esteem, even if you find small ways of doing it. You have to stay physically active because exercise is a major part of keeping balance and self-esteem.

"There's another issue about forced retirement—it's

adjusting your lifestyle to your financial situation. Retirement forces you to make choices, and if you don't choose to bring your lifestyle into line with your resources, you can create huge problems for yourself down the road.

"Reintegration with your partner is another significant issue. It's problematic when you don't have an office to go to and all of a sudden you and your wife are thrown into the same space all the time. You have to talk about it, but there is no getting around the fact that it's an adjustment for both people. That's not easy."

When not pursuing career opportunities, John has dedicated his time to volunteer activities. "Volunteering is a way to still use your skill base and make a contribution. It also provides social interaction and is a way to build your network. A lot of people — especially men — don't think they need social interaction, but it is essential. So I have been working with the American Diabetes Foundation, and I am about to join their board. I am also a business counselor for the local Mexican Consulate. That gives me an opportunity to get out and about and interact with people. I am also on a couple of company boards. One has been around for thirteen years, and the other is just out of the start-up phase. But I don't want to be on any more boards because there is a lot of liability without a lot of authority. So the conclusion I came to is that I don't want any more board assignments. But I do want to do something that is business-oriented. That's who I am."

John believes that recent changes in the workplace will reduce the number of people who are forced into his position in the future. "If all of your achievements are wrapped up in your work and if you have dedicated yourself to your company, you probably never took time to think about your personal life — what you wanted to do beyond your job. And you never spent time developing a network of people outside of work. And when the job is gone that becomes a problem. But I think people are beginning to understand that better now. They don't work for the same companies for as long as we did in the past, and they have found that over the long term they are more dependent upon their contacts and social network than they are on their companies. Younger people today are probably doing a better job of looking out for themselves. And they should.

"I see people my age who are working and happy, but I also see people who are retired and seem to be happy. I haven't spent a lot of time with my retired friends to see what is in their hearts and minds. But I tell anyone who is working not to retire. That shows you what my attitude toward retirement is. Maybe when I am seventy I will have a whole different mental outlook. Maybe I will have coped with this a lot better. Maybe I will feel more financially secure. Maybe I will want to play golf and fly-fish. But I'll have to go through some major changes because I sure can't see myself doing that now. Right now, I know I wouldn't be happy doing that."

T.J. Levitt – *Counting Your Blessings*

T. J. Levitt* grew up in Arkansas and received his bachelor's degree in chemistry and biology from Henderson State University. He was a natural leader and the first member of his family to graduate from college. During the summers, he was a ranger for the U.S. Forest Service. After college and a tour in Vietnam as a Marine Corps pilot, he joined Southwestern Bell, where he worked until AT&T was forced to divest its subsidiaries. He moved to another major telecom firm and advanced to jobs with increasing responsibility until his retirement in 2001.

There was, however, a darker side to T.J.'s story. "Within a year of getting out of the Marine Corps, I had a drinking problem.

* pseudonym

Year after year, it got worse and worse. By June of 1987, I knew I either had to 'end it all' or quit drinking. So I went to AA and was able to quit. My life turned around. I became successful at business and everything started going my way. I was blessed. All of a sudden I was like the golden-haired boy again. I felt renewed."

But there was to be another challenge. "In 1996, when I was an operations director, I was diagnosed with prostate cancer. The doctor told me, 'If you don't do anything, you have about eight years to live and the last two won't be very pretty.' Those were the averages. So I went ahead and had surgery, and when I was recovering I started thinking about what I would do if I really did have only eight years to live. I knew I wanted to make some changes. And one of the things I had always wanted to do was work outside of the United States.

"Six weeks after coming back to work from my disability, my wife, Jan, and I went to China. For three years, I worked on some priority projects, and then I went to Hong Kong and helped our director of operations for Asia Pacific set up the infrastructure in fourteen Asian countries. After I finished doing that, there were no other obvious projects that needed attention. Plus, the telecom bubble had burst, and there were a lot of spending constraints. I was becoming more and more disillusioned. I felt that a lot of the things I was doing were just for political reasons and, really, were a waste of time. I started hating going to work. I finally told my boss that I had done everything I could do, unless he could think of something else. So after four years overseas, we came back to the U.S., even though I knew there probably wouldn't be any jobs open at the company. I was fifty-nine and I had never even thought about retirement. I had just assumed that I would work until I was sixty-five, until the day I had to quit. And, then, I'd leave. So I had no plans when I got back."

The lack of planning was only one of the problems that T.J.

faced upon his return. "The other thing that happened when I was in China was that I started drinking again. Drinking in China's business climate is almost obligatory. You gain 'face' by doing it, and face is very important. For three years, I drank socially, and there was no problem. But when I got to Hong Kong the last year and the job pressures increased, my drinking got heavier and heavier. I have a tremendous capacity to consume alcohol and never appear to be drunk. When we got back to the U.S. and I didn't have anything to do, I absolutely dove into the bottle. And I stayed there from December until August the following year. Everything I looked at was amber or distorted. I didn't want to be around anybody, and nobody wanted to be around me either."

Lack of direction and excessive drinking are a lethal mix. "I had made no plans. I had lost my identity. I didn't know who I was because I had always defined myself by what my job was — rather than by who I am. And the job was gone. I was totally unprepared for retirement and the loss of my identity. I guess I attempted to find it in a bottle. I was drinking 24/7, even getting up at two o'clock in the morning to drink. That year after I retired, I was depressed and bored and couldn't see any way out. I just sank deeper and deeper. And finally I reached the bottom. I weighed fifty pounds more than I do now. I didn't exercise. I didn't eat right. All I did was drink and hide it and lie to all the people around me. I couldn't love anyone. I could say that I did, but when you're that preoccupied with getting your next drink you don't think about other people, much less love them. I was just miserable.

"When I went for my annual physical, the doctor told me I wasn't in any condition to even have an examination. He told me what I already knew; I had to quit drinking. And he gave me some Valium to get me through the first couple of days after I quit. Three days later, I went to my first AA meeting. I was at rock bottom—emotionally, physically, and spiritually. And I told the people at AA that I would do whatever they told me to do. I followed their program, and it worked perfectly. Now I have found happiness. I've gotten my life back again. I know who I am. I found out that I can live life on life's terms.

"I couldn't have asked for anyone to be more supportive than Jan has been. She did not understand what I was going through. No one could have. And I have tried to make amends. I didn't mistreat anybody. I didn't yell or that sort of thing. I just wasn't there. I wasn't there mentally or emotionally. I went inside myself, and I had to do a lot of work to get my life back together. That work took the form of AA's twelve steps, and I worked them really hard. Retirement kicked my butt thoroughly because I was not emotionally prepared for the change and loss of identity. I know I would not be alive today if I had not crawled out of the bottle, crawled back to AA, and really, really worked their program hard.

"I guess I was depressed even before I left Hong Kong, but I didn't know it. My forte had always been helping people develop, and I had a lot of success with that. The paycheck you get is a maintenance thing. You have to have a certain amount of money, but making money is not what turned my crank. I was turned on by seeing people do well and setting the stage for them to develop. But in Hong Kong my job was making recommendations on what the organization had to do to be profitable. So maybe being in a position of always being the one to bring bad news had something to do with my depression. I really don't know. All I know is that I wasn't getting any job satisfaction from what I was doing. I felt I was wasting my time—and other people's time. And this impending question of what to do with the rest of my life just made it worse.

"Retirement was probably the most jarring thing that ever happened to me. I was vulnerable. I was weak. But I have definitely learned some things. If your personal identity is totally tied to your work, you need to get some kind of help when you approach retirement. If you don't, I think you're in for some trouble. It may not be drinking. It may not be drugs. It may not be divorce. It may not be any of those things, but the quality of life that you are going to have in retirement is really going to be affected. I've watched how men try to cope with retirement ever since I got in this situation. Many just seem lost. They don't know what to do with themselves. It seems like they're searching.

"I learned that you shouldn't retire until you have finished your journey in the workplace. And when you do finish that journey, you should unpack and prepare yourself for the next journey. That's a real process. You have to look back and understand where you've been, but you also have to go through the mental exercise of setting new goals and realistic expectations for the future. That's where I missed out. I didn't reflect back on the past, and I didn't have any vision of where I wanted to go next.

"One of the things I missed was that there was no ceremony to mark the change in my life. There was nothing to recognize all the years and contributions, nothing to acknowledge that my status had changed. I'm not much on ceremonies. But I do think that they play a big part when we are going through major life transitions. If I had known that a retirement ceremony was coming up and I had to prepare a five or ten minute speech, the process of preparing that speech would have caused a lot of reflection about what my career had meant to me and what I expected to be doing in the future. I think that would have helped a lot. Retirement is a passage, and it's important that you and the people around you acknowledge that passage."

T.J. is extraordinarily thankful for surviving all that he put himself through. "I feel grateful. I feel good physically, emotionally, and spiritually. I am blessed. I don't know if anybody could ask for any more. I can't tell you how good the last year has been in comparison to the year that preceded it. The good news is that there is a God. The bad news is that it isn't me. That's a rude awakening to a lot of us; egos are a huge problem for alcoholics. You've got to get outside yourself. I am now ready to give to others, but I wasn't before. The only way for me to keep my sobriety is to be working with others. In helping them, they will ask questions that will make me look objectively at myself.

"I tried working part-time, and I was successful at it. But that has no place in my life anymore. There was no fulfillment in selling air conditioners. So I don't want to go back to work. I'm okay financially, and I have things to offer as a volunteer that are more important to me now. I have been an extremely fortunate person. I was a forest ranger. I survived as a Marine Corps pilot in Vietnam. I've lived in twenty-five different states and a couple of foreign countries. I have three sons who have grown into fine individuals in spite of me. I've been an executive. I survived prostate cancer. And I've been saved two times from my own self-destructive behavior. I have been blessed with so much. And I have done nothing to deserve it. So now it's payback time. I find that doing volunteer work, part of it with AA, is fulfilling. Helping others will be a big part of my life for as long as I live. I want to know that I have done something worthwhile, that I've contributed. I guess that I'm back to doing what I love—helping people develop and grow."

Peg Zarlengo –
Your Happiness Hinges on Your Decisions

PEG ZARLENGO'S NEED TO EXCEL was inherited from her father, a workaholic and senior executive at Union Pacific Railroad. Peg became a banker, and she loved her work. During her career with a regional bank she managed a branch, headed the workout division, and oversaw a business-banking hub. Her husband, Vince, was a CPA and attorney who was similarly absorbed with his profession. They didn't have children, but instead set their sights on early retirement. The transition came sooner than planned but took an unexpected turn.

"Our life plan had always been to retire when Vince was fifty-five and I was fifty-three. We ended up doing it three years earlier than that because he was burned out on testifying as an expert witness and decided to take a sabbatical. But as he was thinking through what he was going to do next, he couldn't figure out what to do with himself at home. He ended up going to his office even during his sabbatical. So, he decided to go back to work part-time. Now he provides litigation support services to the attorneys in his office, but it isn't year-round and his schedule is flexible. We have the freedom to do whatever we want whenever we want.

"I thought about retiring for three years before I finally did it. But I had a hard time getting up the courage. I was a workaholic. I never seemed to have time for anything but work. And work was such a part of my identity. When people met me at parties, they would know within thirty seconds that I was a banker because I thought that really defined who I was, and I wasn't sure who I would be if I didn't have that. Even though I knew I didn't want to continue at the bank, I couldn't think of another career that I was excited to leap into or that I was qualified for.

"It was very frightening when I started getting serious about retiring. Even though I wasn't totally happy at the bank, I started wondering what I would do if I retired and didn't like it. Finally, a friend of mine said, 'Peg, it's just a job, and it's not the only one in the whole wide world. I think you are probably good enough that if you don't like being retired, you can find another one. And if you don't like retirement, you'll know that, and you will be happier when you do go back to work.'

"During the three years that I was thinking about quitting, I also thought about all of the things I would do if I retired. I was afraid that I wouldn't have enough to do, that I would be bored, and that I would feel sorry for myself. But after I quit, I over-committed myself. I didn't realize that people sort of prey on you when they think that you may have free time. They ask you to volunteer to do all kinds of things. It may be that you are talented, but a lot of it is also that you are seen as available.

"So I ended up on a couple of boards, a community board and a homeowners' association board. I joined a garden club. I took art classes. I played golf. One of the first things I joined was an investment club. I did that about a year and a half before I quit working. It was a great way to get to know a group of twelve women in my neighborhood. I knew that I could offer some expertise in terms of being able to read financial statements. It also gave me connections that led to other activities with them.

"The first year of retirement I was busier than when I worked. My schedule was impossible. I had too many meetings and things to do. Then I thought, 'This isn't fun. This is too much like work, except I am not getting paid to do it.' That really helped me to better understand what I wanted. And I started dropping the activities that didn't satisfy me. When I started peeling things off and focusing on what I really wanted to do, I found out that I liked having some time to myself. I had never had that opportunity before.

"One thing I am doing that I enjoy—and is really reward-ing—is being a clown. I am part of a clown ministry. We go visit people in nursing homes or independent residences who are no longer able to go to church. During the month of their birthday, we go to cheer them up. We dress up as clowns and take them cookies and flowers. What we do when we get there depends on who they are and what they will enjoy. Sometimes we sing. Sometimes we dance. Sometimes we play games. Sometimes they just want to talk because they are lonely. We do whatever will bring them some happiness. When I tell people about this they often comment that it is wonderful that we do that for the seniors. And maybe that's right. But it's even more wonderful for me because I totally step out of my normal role. When you're a clown, you're not a person. You're imaginary. You're an entertainer. It's fun. It makes you think about things in a different way. And the reactions of some of the people are just great. One guy was so happy when we came to surprise him that he jumped up, and with his hands still on his walker, clicked his heels together.

"When I retired the thing that I was most looking forward to was getting up in the morning, having my coffee, and thinking about what I wanted to do. Getting up, without having something that I had to rush off to do. And, I guess, for some people that is perfect. But, as it turns out, that does not work for me—at least not on a regular basis. Now, the few times that happens it is a big treat. But I know that if I didn't have a lot of things going on, I could start feeling sorry for myself or like I wasn't a real person anymore.

"After a career in which I considered myself to be pretty successful, the hardest part of retirement is not feeling really competent or proficient at much of anything. I'm a beginning artist. I am a beginning clown. I am not good at golf. I have to keep reminding myself that you don't become an expert at anything overnight. If it was easy to be great at any of these things, what would be the point of the challenge? In fact, if it was easy, it probably wouldn't be very fun. So the flip side is that I am doing things that are stimulating for me. And I am really enjoying myself. I don't want another career. The thing I love the most about being retired is the freedom, the flexibility of time. I don't want to *have* to do anything. I want the choices to be mine."

Liz Snowden – *A Road Less Traveled*

LIZ SNOWDEN HAS CHARGED THROUGH LIFE. In the ten years after she graduated from Stanford with a psychology degree, she worked for Price Waterhouse, became a CPA, earned her MBA from Harvard, and worked as a product manager for Carnation Foods. She then jumped at the opportunity to become a director of marketing for a small medical referral service company. That ultimately led to helping Joe Tallman form and build a start-up medical software and services company that, after three mergers, became part of McKesson Corporation. Liz married Joe in 1993, and their daughter was born five years later. They retired after the McKesson merger and are now financially secure. They are thoroughly enjoying retirement, but not every issue has been resolved.

"Looking back, I don't know how we ever kept our house together after we got married. There was so much going on. We both worked full-time — long, long hours. Joe had been married before, and when we got married, there were four teenage step-kids who lived with us half-time. During that time neither Joe nor I did anything for ourselves. Life was just working and being with the kids. That was it."

Until then, balancing her roles had never been an issue. "In the first part of my career, I didn't have anything to balance. I didn't get married until I was thirty-six. And then all of a sudden I had step-kids, and there was a balance issue because we needed to meet their needs. It was different years later when my own daughter was born because it became even more of an emotional issue.

"When I was working, I defined myself in terms of my job. Most people do. If you had asked me twenty years ago, I would have said that I was not going to have kids. That was not in the picture. I had no interest in that at all. But it's amazing how that has changed. Now, I have a five-year-old. I'm a mom. Somehow, I lived the first half of my life like my dad and now I'm living the second half like my mom."

Having been so focused on her work, Liz was initially eager to get back to the office after her daughter was born. "I remember when I first went back to work, I was really determined to get back into it. People told me, 'Just wait a year; you won't want to be here.' I didn't believe them, but they were right. The older she got, and the cuter she was, and the harder she cried when I left to go to work, the more important it became for me to spend more time with her. I really feel blessed to have been able to do all of the career things that I wanted to do. And now I have the freedom to spend a lot of time with her."

After the McKesson merger, Liz worked three days a week for a while and then retired. But despite her desire to spend more time with her daughter, there was still a period of adjustment. "At first, I felt guilty that I was taking so much time for myself. It seemed weird. There was no one trying to get in touch with me. I'd look at the computer and there weren't eighty-five emails waiting for me to respond, nothing in the in-box. And I'd think, 'Is this computer working?' In fact, I would probably be working again if I was not a mom. Maybe it's the Protestant work ethic, but I need to be involved. I feel a need to contribute. And I often feel like I should be doing more than I am. I feel that I have been blessed with abilities to do things and that I shouldn't let them go to waste.

"One of the things I missed the most was the group of people we worked with. That was one of the really great things about going to work every day. It was fun to be around bright, thoughtful people who were well meaning in what they were doing and who were working together to solve problems. That piece is now missing, at least in the intense way that I had before.

"I know that a lot of women are concerned about how they

and their husbands will get along when they retire and spend more time together. But that hasn't been a big issue for me because Joe and I met at work, and we have always spent a lot of time together. In fact, it's easier now because there isn't the same pressure we had when we were working together. We each do our own thing.

"When I was working, I had no time for myself. But I always had a 'to do' list that stayed there for years. One thing was to take a painting class; another was to take a creative writing class. When I left work, I started signing up for classes. Now I've taken all of the art classes that I could find, some of them twice. I'm still trying to figure out whether I am ever going to be able to paint well. I don't think so, but at least I enjoy doing it.

"I also knew that I wanted to be personally involved with a non-profit. During the years of working, I never had a chance to give anything back, other than to write a check. Now I'm on the board of the Family Learning Center. It's a wonderful charity here in town that works with low-income families by helping them achieve self-sufficiency through education. I probably spend ten hours a week working on that. It's also something that I can get my daughter involved with so that she will learn how to help other people. But still, while I feel good about helping this charity, I keep thinking that I have the potential to do more. In some ways I feel like I am a little kid again, asking that question, 'What do I want to do when I grow up?'

"One of the things on my 'to do' list is to decide whether I want to get a Ph.D. and maybe go into teaching. My interest in psychology keeps coming back, particularly the question about what makes organizations work, or not work. We went through three mergers, and we acquired three other companies. The whole idea of corporate culture is something that people don't understand very well. But I am not sure that I want to commit the time that would be needed to get that Ph.D.

"I am loving life. It's not a typical retirement because I have a young child instead of grandchildren. But I think that one of the keys to a good retirement is that you have to want to be there. I've heard stories about people who have faced mandatory retirement and don't have a clue about what they want to do next. Fortunately, that is not a problem for me. But you have to be involved. That is still a struggle for me. I think that I have felt a little bit isolated, and I want to connect with other people a bit more."

Frank Day – *Just Keep Rolling*

FRANK DAY RETIRED IN 1995, but he hasn't been able to stop working yet. In his early seventies, he just keeps rolling.

Frank escaped from Harvard with an undergraduate degree in English, an MBA, and an open mind. His inquisitiveness and energy came mostly from his mother, whose background included retailing, promotion, advertising, television, and real estate development. He grew up in Oak Park, Illinois, across the street from Ernest Hemingway's childhood home.

After stints as a bartender, hot dog vendor, doughnut retailer, and Burger King franchisee, Frank opened a trend-setting family restaurant. The course was set. Today, he is the driving force behind Concept Restaurants, Inc.; Rock Bottom Restaurants, Inc.; Black Hawk Gaming & Development Co.; and Rockies Brewing Co.; among others. Together, his hospitality businesses employ 8,000 people. He has had a lot of fun—and stress—along the way.

Frank's largest investment is in Rock Bottom, which went public in 1994. A year later, he cut back his involvement in the company and retired to a new home in the Virgin Islands. But by 1997, Rock Bottom was having problems and takeover artists were circling, searching for ways to buy the company at a depressed price. Frank would have none of that. "I didn't want another dog to get my bone." He raised the necessary money, took Rock Bottom private, and has been active on a part-time basis ever since.

"When I cut back in 1995, I had the naïve vision that the company would grow and grow, and over time I would unload my stock. It could have happened, but it didn't. Then I found that as a major stockholder I didn't have liquidity. There wasn't much trading of the stock going on, and I had to do something. In the future, it shouldn't take more than half of my time, maybe less. But thinking through what we should be doing with the business and where we should be going takes a lot of concentration and energy.

"Meanwhile I get involved in all sorts of other things. I am a self-confessed 'dealaholic.' I'm always looking for new investments. Some of the deals turn out fine. Others don't. But for some reason when my life starts to become simple I get uncomfortable. So I complicate it again—loading up with more than I can handle.

"Work and play are intermixed for me. I've never been able to separate them. I like to be with people, and I've got 8,000 of them. I have always liked to party, and I'm in the bar business. What's a better place for me to be? A lot of my social activities are blended into my job. I like being around people who want to do things well and who want to achieve. And achieving is what life is about—at least it has been a big factor for me. I feel sorry for the people who don't get that wonderful sense of satisfaction from life.

"In the future, I'll keep doing deals. I don't think I will ever get to the point that I just do nothing. I like keeping my stress level under control and I have a pretty good lifestyle, but since I retired I am busier than ever in terms of being scheduled. We travel a lot and between trips there are so many things that I have to get done. The restaurant business never stops. So I don't have a lot of unstructured time.

"About twenty or thirty years ago, my view of life changed. If you think of plotting life on a graph, I started in the lower left-hand corner and I saw myself moving up and to the right. Somewhere along the line I realized that life isn't like that, or it shouldn't be. So I adopted a different three-dimensional model of life. It's a bowl, and the bowl has a hole in the bottom. I'm a marble rolling around this bowl. You go too fast and you go over the edge. You quit and you drop through the hole. The message is you have to keep going. Every time around may have a different trajectory. There may be some déjà vu, but it's a little different than it was last time. So my goal is to just keep rolling and watching the scenery as it goes by.

"I don't want to be bored, I like the challenges along the way, and I want to be able to leave a legacy behind me as I go. One of the legacies is to see that the key people who have helped me on the journey do well. They have worked so hard. Some have worked for me for twenty-five or thirty years. And I want to make sure that it works for them.

"I have had a lot of free time to fool around over the years, perhaps because I have been captain of my own ship. And since I was able to do that, I don't have any huge compulsion to kick back and relax now. I don't need to stop and smell the roses because I have been doing that all along. I developed a philosophy years ago that you better smell them as you go, or you might miss out. And the older you get and the more you live day-by-day and week-by-week, the more you realize that this is the right way to go.

"I am enjoying this stage of my life. I'm in good health, and I try to be conscious of it. I've tried to develop a reasonably healthy lifestyle. I watch what I eat and exercise all I can. I love to hike, bike, ski, fish, and kayak. I don't know whether it is

maturing or whatever, but I don't get as upset about things as I did before. I take things as they come. It seems to me that if you can keep your health, keep your mental faculties, keep jerks out of your life, and just keep rolling, life should be pretty good. Just do that because one day you won't be rolling anymore.

"I also try to keep a hand in charitable and non-profit activities, which is actually where I would like to spend more of my time — and also put in more money. I set up a private foundation that focuses on hunger and the homeless. We have a program that feeds people at Christmastime in a bunch of different states. That's what my wife, Gina, and I do on Christmas day now. We get in the serving line and serve the people. It's really rewarding. We also do a lot of fundraising things for charities like the MS Walk. I give some scholarships and am also a contributor to the St. Croix Foundation. I want to spend more time on charity work and gradually put together a program to give back most of what I have accumulated.

"At this stage, I want to keep my life as pleasant as possible. I want to be able to spend time with the people who I want to be with and put the people I don't want to be with in the rear view mirror as fast as possible. Being able to do that makes life so much nicer. The real stressful times in life are because of jerks. So, I want to avoid them.

"I have seen several people in retirement shed their skin and grow a new one. In some way, they break their routine and shift gears. By relaunching, they renew themselves and rediscover their passion. And when that passion runs its course, they may do it all over again. So they never get bored. The people who are bored are bored because they let it happen. Boredom comes from within. I don't think that I am one of those people who will shed his skin. But I enjoy what I am doing, I hope to keep active, and I don't think I will ever be bored."

Observations about Making the Transition

AT THE BEGINNING OF THIS CHAPTER, we set out to determine *who* has difficulties making the transition to retirement, *why* they have those difficulties, and *what* can be done about it. Based on comments from people in the Retirement Puzzle Cohort, it turns out that the *who* is determined largely by the *why*. Those who are most likely to have transitional problems tend to be more focused on what they are leaving behind than on what they are moving toward. People who experience these difficulties usually have some of the following characteristics:

- A single-minded commitment to their work

- Identities that are tied to their jobs

- Limited interests beyond their careers

- Social lives that are closely integrated with their working lives

- Challenging, high-visibility jobs

- No established retirement goals or expectations

- Retirement forced on them before they have mentally prepared

- Feelings of incompleteness because career goals have not been met

- Inadequate financial security

- Major personal problems after they retire

- Few friends

- Incomplete relationships at home

Each of these contributes to transitional problems, and the more of these characteristics an individual has, the more likely that person is to experience difficulties. And those difficulties will affect whomever he or she lives with.

Historically, these characteristics have been more descriptive of men than they have been of women, and generally men encounter more transitional difficulties. Traditional female social behavior features social interaction, cooperation, wide-ranging interests, and multiple roles. In fact, one of the problems that women typically face during their careers is balancing those multiple roles. By eliminating or reducing one of the roles, retirement may partially solve that problem. By contrast, men are often more independent, less social, more competitive, and single-minded in focus. In fact, many men are so work-focused that they view time devoted to diversionary issues as time wasted or even a source of guilt. Men — and women who have an intense work orientation — may find that retirement creates, rather than solves, problems.

For people who do have difficulty making the transition, the overriding question is, "What can be done about it?" The answer most frequently articulated by people in the Retirement Puzzle Cohort is to avoid boredom and stay involved. That may be adequate advice for some people, but for others it simply prompts another question, "Stay involved with what?" We are unlikely to devote our energy to golf — or any other activity — in retirement if we previously had little interest in it. And filling our schedule with activities that we don't care about is not a solution. We need to find something that will rekindle the passion and excitement we previously found in our work.

This was exactly the dilemma I faced when I retired. My identity had been wrapped around my business, and I didn't have a long list of other activities I was eager to pursue. I found that I needed to discard my old identity and replace it with a new one that I could adopt with equal enthusiasm and energy. Becoming an author, researching and writing this book, was my solution. I had always enjoyed writing, and written reports were a major part of my profession. This book provided me with the challenge and mission I needed to make the transition and still feel alive.

Each of us must find a solution that meets our unique needs. We may find it through religion, volunteering, education, entrepreneurship, travel, athletics, art, music, environmentalism, woodworking, mentoring, politics, or any other endeavor that truly interests us. It may be a mixture of some of the above. But it must include something for which we have a passion. Having a passion is the difference between being occupied and being exhilarated. It is a major step toward getting the most out of the rest of our lives.

We have seen that many people who have adjusted well to retirement find their passion by giving something back to society, usually through volunteering for a worthy cause. By doing so, they acknowledge their good fortune and express their appreciation. This has the added benefit of providing them with a greater sense of meaning and purpose.

People who do not have a clear vision of how they want to spend their time may be well advised to follow T. J.'s advice and seek professional help in sorting through the changes occurring in their lives. However, whether we receive assistance or work through the process alone, we can start to rediscover ourselves by answering these questions:

- Who am I in the absence of my job?

- What motivates me?

- What is important?

- What am I leaving behind?

- What do I love doing?

- What are my strengths?

- What are my weaknesses?

- What do I choose to avoid?

The answers to these questions can lead to a personal vision of how we want to live our retirement lives.

To achieve a successful transition, we must first let go of the past. The people who are happiest are those who don't dwell on yesterday or fret about tomorrow. They have learned to accept the past for what it is—history. And they have developed a vision of the future—how they would like their lives to unfold. But they live in the present. Their approach is to be adaptable, positive, and involved. And their days are full and rewarding because they are committed to living the way they choose to live.

THE THIRD CHALLENGE:
Managing Physical, Mental, and Spiritual Health

(If you don't breathe, nothing else matters!)

 EARLIER, BILL FISCHER WARNED US about his four perils of retirement. He has another observation that is just as thought-provoking. "Remember how naïve you were when you were a teenager? How you knew that you were bulletproof? Well, do you realize that most of us are still naïve and still acting carelessly in our sixties and seventies? Retirees do not plan for the deterioration of their health, even though it is inevitable. They are in denial and don't want to think about it. This is a major problem because deteriorating health is unavoidable. And when physical deterioration — or even mental deterioration—happens to them, they are totally unprepared. It's a shame!"

Sometimes the truth hurts, but it is the truth nonetheless. Happiness and fulfillment are linked to our physical, mental, and spiritual health, which is why eroding health is our third retirement challenge. There is a great deal that we can do to promote health and well-being, and by taking appropriate actions we will improve our retirement experience. At the same time, aging and mortality are inescapable, and to ensure lasting happiness and fulfillment they must also be addressed properly. Thus, we must take better care of ourselves *and* prepare to manage expected and unexpected changes. The people in this chapter have successfully confronted these issues and provide sound advice to help us cope with the inevitable.

Nancy Smalley – *Lifestyle Matters*

NANCY SMALLEY BELIEVES that a healthy lifestyle is the key to a fulfilling life and has lived her life accordingly. She is a nutritionist who is constantly challenging herself mentally and physically. With talent and discipline, Nancy also has become a world-class athlete.

Nancy was born and raised in Detroit. In 1947, she graduated from Michigan State University with a degree in Foods and Nutrition. Before raising her children, she was a researcher at the United States Department of Agriculture in Washington D.C. When her kids had grown, she decided it was time for a new challenge. "I thought, 'Many women blossom after their kids have grown, and I've probably got another thirty years to live. What am I going to do with myself?' I decided I would go back to school and get a master's degree. But it wasn't that easy. I had to go back to college and redo my undergraduate science courses because so much had changed since I had been in school. I had to take two chemistry classes, physiology, algebra, and nutrition classes before I could even be admitted to graduate school.

"I wasn't sure I could do all of the memory work that was necessary, but I did. I think your brain is like your muscles. You use it or you lose it. The challenge was great, and I got along just fine. At first, I didn't take full course loads because I didn't want to push myself so hard that I wouldn't do well. After I got admitted to graduate school, I did take a fairly full load and graduated with a master's in nutritional consulting in 1988. Anyway, I did well and made a lot of friends that I still keep in touch with. The whole experience was just great."

Her graduate program included courses in transpersonal psychology, wellness, and nutrition. Many of the courses were taught by working professionals, including medical doctors, nurses, chiropractors, naturopaths, and acupuncturists. After graduating, she went to work with a naturopath teaching his clients about diet and nutrition. "In this country we over-medicate, and many people are coming to realize that there are alternatives that make more sense. Naturopaths have four years post-graduate medical training. They know about drugs, but they don't use them. They focus on lifestyle changes, detox, and diet. If your body is treated right, it knows what to do. But if you overload it with things it can't handle, there will be problems.

"In fact, medical doctors are becoming more cautious about how they prescribe drugs. At a seminar I went to recently, I heard a pharmacist say that he believes patients usually should not take more than three drugs at one time. He said that they can figure out the interactions among three drugs, but it gets much more difficult as the number goes up from there. On top of that, a lot of older people often can't keep more than three drugs straight or take them all properly.

"I know a lot about nutrition and how to eat well. But one diet doesn't fit all people. Some people do well as vegetarians and others need meat. Some do well with dairy products and for others they are terrible. Some can drink coffee and others can't. You have to learn what is right for you. There is also a need to supplement your diet, but I don't think that people should try to figure out how to supplement their own diets. They should go to someone who knows about supplements. Then, based on blood tests and other factors, they should take what is appropriate for them.

"Now we have a lot more awareness about how we can use nutrition to support the body. Why take drugs with all of their side effects when you can support your body naturally? If you get so sick that you are in crisis, you need traditional medical care. We are never going to get away from that. But even the medical profession is finally getting on the nutritional band-wagon because the general public is so aware of the importance of nutrition.

"Nutrition is not the only solution. Even when you have your nutrition under control and are properly nourishing your body, you still can't be really healthy unless you are at least somewhat physically active. You sure don't need to do as much as I do, but you should do at least a moderate amount of exercise. Your body is not going to be healthy unless you use it to some degree. And the more you use it—within reason—the better. But there are limits; you can also push yourself too hard."

Apparently, Nancy has pushed herself hard enough! When she was younger she was a skier and golfer. But she wanted to add aerobic exercise to her routine and started running when she turned fifty-four. In 1981, she decided to compete. The rest, as they say, is history. Since then, she has won more than twenty gold medals in National and World Masters Track and Field Championships. In 1995, she was the national champion in six different distances (the 400, 800, 1,500, 3,000 meters indoors and 5,000 and 10,000 outdoors). She has competed around the U.S. as well as in South Africa, Australia, and China. With three other Americans, she set the standing world record for the 4x400 relay for women seventy and older.

"I work out six or seven days a week. I run four days a week for about an hour and fifteen minutes, and I cross-train the other days. But the key is that I know when to back off. That is why I have lasted as long as I have. There is a group of about fif-teen to eighteen men and women in our fifties, sixties, seventies, and eighties who have run together for quite a while. I just love to train with them. So, I don't take a lot of time off unless I am injured.

"The physical activity also helps me stay mentally alert. Researchers are learning a lot more about what it takes to keep your brain healthy, as well as your body. Your brain is going to work better if you feed it and get enough oxygen to it. That is one of the reasons why aerobic exercise is important, mentally and physically."

Nancy is living a lifestyle that will most likely lead to prolonged physical and mental health. She does not smoke, controls her weight and blood pressure, is conscientious about her diet and takes prescribed dietary supplements, gets aerobic and strength exercise regularly, is socially involved, and challenges herself mentally. She also is actively engaged in helping others. "I stay involved. Lots of people know that I am a nutritionist, and I am on several committees that make use of my expertise. I still go to seminars, and my athletic friends often ask me questions. I really enjoy being able to help people learn how to live healthier lives."

In so many ways, Nancy is a terrific role model for us. It is unlikely that most of us will closely follow her demanding regimen, but the more we emulate the example she has set, the more apt we are to have mental and physical health. Unfortunately, there are no guarantees, as Jim Neher will attest.

Jim Neher — *A Renewed Perspective on Life*

JIM NEHER GREW UP in Flushing, New York, and New Canaan, Connecticut. His father was the syndicated cartoonist who drew "Life's Like That," a strip that ran in about 500 newspapers. After college and a stint in the Navy, Jim married Judy and gravitated to the advertising business in San Francisco. He loved the work and the challenges, but it was consuming and intense. Jim remembers the time one of his young daughters said to him, "Daddy, when are you going to come home and play with us?" It was a wake-up call, and Jim realized that he had to make a change. He redefined his work priorities: to be his own boss, have time with his family, and make a good income.

Jim moved on to become a State Farm Insurance agent for the next twenty-seven years. "The job I chose gave me what I needed. It gave me time to spend with Judy and the kids. It gave me the money I needed to live comfortably. But it was not something that I truly enjoyed. It's a frustrating business. Even though the insurance industry is very helpful and provides a great service, insurance companies won't work together to build a better image. So, the industry's reputation isn't what it could be. And claims got to be much tougher in the last few years because all of the insurance companies were tightening their belts. I probably spent eighty percent of my time trying to work out claims for my clients. It was not something that I wanted to do for the rest of my life. So I decided to retire when I was sixty-two. I had my finances pretty well planned, and I sent State Farm a letter of resignation."

Things don't always work out as anticipated. "I had a stroke several months before I was scheduled to retire. We were at our vacation home up in the mountains. I was sitting on the sofa, and I remember feeling a flow of blood in my head. Something was going on that wasn't right, and I told Judy about it. The next thing I remember, the ambulance attendants were carrying me down the stairs. From that point on I don't remember much. It was the kind of stroke that only a small percentage of people survive.

"In the hospital, Judy thought I was dying. I remember someone pounding on my chest. Then they said, 'We're going to have to tap his skull.' I remember having double vision because of the build-up of blood in my head. They ended up putting a shunt in to relieve the pressure. I was in intensive care for almost three weeks, and I don't remember much about that. I do know that I had some strange or delusional thoughts. In intensive care the lights are on all the time, and you don't sleep. You can get paranoid. When I was finally released, I rehabilitated at another hospital, relearning how to think, walk, and talk.

"When I went into therapy I wasn't functioning very well. It was like part of my brain was numbed. I could understand what was going on around me, and I knew what I wanted to say. But I had trouble remembering the words to express myself. I also had trouble with my balance and my reactions. It took two weeks of therapy just to get my balance back. They gave me a series of tests to see how my brain was working. Before I finally went home, I had to pass a driver's test at the hospital to make sure my reactions were okay.

"They think it was high blood pressure that caused the stroke. I was overweight, and I lost more than thirty pounds when I was in the hospital. But following the stroke, my diet didn't change at all. I just kept eating, and I gained about fifty pounds. I was huge. I was eating everything that didn't eat me. Honestly, I probably felt sorry for myself and decided that I was going to do whatever would make me happy. But I finally caught on, and Judy agreed to go on a diet with me. Now, we are eating salads and smaller portions, and avoiding carbohydrates. And we are going to continue it. I call it a diet, but really it's just a different way of eating. It's not using food as a reward.

"I did go through a bit of depression after the stroke. That was a big change for me because I have always been optimistic. The weight gain probably had something to do with it. I went to a neural psychologist. He said, 'It is normal to realize that you are not perfect. You are going to be fine.' Depression can be a cycle; you get into a critical frame of mind, and it's hard to get out of it. You just have to find a way to work yourself through it. If you start thinking positive thoughts, they'll build on themselves. And you can get yourself out of it.

"My energy level could be a bit better now, but that is the result of some of the pills I am taking. So I take naps in the afternoon. I used to hate to do that, but now I almost look forward to it because it gives me my energy back. If I could get off some of the medications I am taking, I wouldn't have to take the naps, but right now that is not an option."

Jim's life-threatening experience affected him deeply. "When I wake up in the morning, I'm glad I'm still around. I understand that I am not going to live forever, and that has changed how I look at things. I've slowed down. I think I am more patient and understanding. I appreciate Judy a lot more now. She is a very warm, caring person. Very nurturing. And I appreciate the smaller things. I enjoy just watching people in shopping centers. I like to watch what they do and how different they are. I think I am more aware of things going on around me and about where I am in my life. I am more cautious than I used to be. For years I played racquetball, but that was the only exercise I got. Now I work out three or four times a week on the treadmill or with weights.

"I keep myself pretty busy working around the house and in the yard. I read a lot more than I used to. I am starting to play a lot more golf. Two times a month I go to the first grade class my daughter teaches. I help the kids read and work with different subjects. It's fun. They are cute little kids. I know that I eventually want to get involved as a volunteer, but I haven't figured out what that is going to look like. I know that I don't want to be a fundraiser. I don't want to 'hit up' my old clients and say, 'Send me money.'"

Jim has learned to appreciate life and relish moments that before his stroke may have seemed inconsequential. "Now, every once in a while, I find myself speeding out of control. But I have learned to calm myself down—and enjoy the moment and my surroundings. That's a big change for me."

Mary Ide – *Wellness Works*

MARY IDE WAS BORN IN WYOMING, where her ancestors had homesteaded when it was still a territory. During her life she has experienced the advantages and disadvantages of that independent, Western heritage.

Mary grew up in Casper and Cheyenne, and most of her relatives were ranchers. When she went to college, she majored in English literature. Mary and Bob Ide married in 1957, and shortly after their third child was born Mary's life took an unexpected turn for which she was totally unprepared. "When my youngest son was two years old, I had what they now call severe anxiety attacks. My heart would start racing. I would pass out. I got to the point I couldn't eat or go out, but staying home didn't help either. I was out of control and almost non-functional. I was in fear twenty-four hours a day, and I knew that there was no reason for it. Everyone would say, 'Pull yourself up by your bootstraps' or 'Look at all the other people having trouble. Why are you complaining?' But those comments didn't help at all. They just increased my sense of helplessness. I knew perfectly well that nothing in the world was threatening me, but that had nothing to do with how I was feeling.

"I ended up receiving psychiatric help and was able to pull out of it with a combination of psychotherapy, some medication, a lot of reading, and honestly facing my problems. It was a hard two years, but I finally learned that the solution has to be internal. You have to realize that nobody else is going to change your life for you. You have to develop a positive attitude and let it grow. You have to understand that you will only get as much out of life as you are willing to put in. Fortunately, I was able to do that, but not everybody can. It was like going through war, the worst experience in the world. But once I had done that and survived, I felt like I could handle anything.

"After I got well, I had a lot of empathy for people who had mental problems. So, I worked as a volunteer counselor at a mental health center. Later, I started doing some non-traditional training and neuro-linguistic programming. Then I went to work as a counselor in the Corrections Department at the Justice Center. I was dealing one-on-one with people who had gotten themselves in trouble with the law—mostly misdemeanors, DUIs, and spousal abuse. I had the feeling that I was making a real contribution."

Shortly after Mary and Bob reached their sixties, Bob wanted to downsize. "My husband was ready to move out of our house. The house was too big, the kids were gone, and there was too much stuff. He wanted to move to Frasier Meadows (a large continuous care community) because he had been so impressed by my mother doing it voluntarily and taking the decision out of our hands. There are so many people who resist moving out of their homes, even when their health keeps declining. It is really hard on their kids, and Bob didn't want to do that to ours. I wasn't sure that I was ready for such a change, but I got to thinking, 'Do I want to move out of this great big house and then have to move again in ten or fifteen years?' So when we visited Frasier Meadows and I saw the gorgeous view and all of the benefits, I agreed.

"It was not too long after that decision that I became ill. We had barely moved in here. I couldn't put things away. I couldn't move. I couldn't do anything! I wondered if it was stress or what the problem was, and the doctors couldn't figure it out. Finally one doctor diagnosed rheumatoid arthritis and put me on several medications. I took a steroid for about three years. As soon as I started taking it, I immediately got better. But steroids deplete calcium from your system, and I was on all other kinds of drugs too. I was worried about the long-term effects of it all, and I knew I had to find another solution.

"I was one of the first people to join the wellness program here. I started exercising. Then, I added workouts in the swimming pool and a yoga class and a Pilates class. I got a massage once a week. I am now down to only one medication. I am completely off steroids and have been for almost three years. I only go to the rheumatoid arthritis doctor for maintenance. He is absolutely amazed by my progress. I keep saying I was misdiagnosed, and he keeps saying. 'Maybe you're in remission.' Well, my remission keeps going on! And I believe it's the wellness program here that has made the difference.

"I really thought that I would be wheelchair-bound. And if I had been living in a house, there's no way I could have gotten into a car to go do all the activities that I think have made the difference. So, moving in here has changed my life. I am on four or five committees. I know almost everyone who lives here. I write for the paper. I do a lot. And I know that if I was still living in my house, I would either still be taking those drugs or be totally isolated by now.

"We are pretty young to be here, but I am really happy. I now know that I was in the right place to get my health under control and keep it under control. I also know I eat better here than I would otherwise. I still cook a lot, but we have to eat some meals in the community dining room each month. And when we eat there they have all kinds of vegetables and fruits and salads to pick from.

"I think that people should reevaluate what continuing care facilities like this really are. Everybody thinks about nursing homes and how depressing they seem. They make people think about their own mortality. But this place is so different. It's amazing. The people here have been all over the world, written books, and have so many incredible stories to tell. Living here is about learning how to live the last part of your life. It's about learning how to address all the issues that have to be addressed. And when you are surrounded by other people who are also addressing those, it is so much easier.

"But if you wait until too late to move in, it can be depressing. The way we did it, we thought of this move as the beginning of the last third of our lives. If you wait until you're sick, you just think of it as the end. The thing people have to understand is that, whether they like it or not, at some point they are going to face deteriorating health. We think you are much better off facing that early, rather than when it's too late.

"Another thing is that moving here was like buying an insurance policy for our kids. They don't have to decide what to do as we get older or experience other health problems. And our kids visit us now more than they did before, because their kids love it. They get to pick and choose what they want in the dining room. They love the elevators and the swimming pool. They love to go across the street to the park. And our kids know that when they come I am not having to slave and cook for them. So it is just perfect. It has been nothing but a plus for us."

Mary is totally committed to maintaining mental awareness and acuity as she ages. "Staying interested in what is going on in the world is important. Being involved with other people and interested in what they are doing is also important. I think that one of the traps people can get into is taking themselves too seriously. That can lead to depression and stress. You don't want to go there. So, I think humor is an important part of life. I am reading more than I had time for in the past and am forcing myself to read some things that are more challenging or stretching. I am also a crossword puzzle freak and that helps keep me more alert."

Mary believes that people should do a better job of looking to the future. "A lot of people just don't want to think about their long-term health or mortality. It's easier and less threatening for them to just think, 'If I get that feeble, I'll just die.' But that isn't what happens. So, people ought to take more time thinking realistically about the future. I was only eight years old when my fourteen-year-old brother died, and from that point on I have always understood that we are all mortal. It is possible that early experience led to my personal crisis when my kids were young. But that experience is now helping me to deal with the problems we all face as we get older."

Ken Myers – *A Young Attitude*

THE SPANISH INFLUENZA that killed as many as forty million people internationally and 675,000 in the U.S. was raging when Ken Myers was born in 1918. His mother contracted the disease and had a temperature of 106 the day he arrived. Ken entered the world with boils covering his hands and arms, but he survived. His tenacity would be challenged many more times.

When he was young, Ken developed a love for music that he has maintained throughout his life. Before World War II, he played with various dance bands, and during the war he played first trumpet in the First Army Band. In December 1944, as the Allied troops were marching across Europe toward the eventual defeat of Germany, the band was scheduled to play a decoration ceremony for a new general in a small town on the Luxembourg-German border. The timing was less than ideal, as it turned out to be the beginning of the Battle of the Bulge. The German advance was unexpected and massive, and it resulted in the capture of thousands of U.S. soldiers, including Ken. After his capture, Ken was wounded by an Allied bomb in a friendly-fire attack. He had to march for six days with a collapsed lung and shrapnel in his foot. During the next four months, he lost eighty pounds as a prisoner of war. Ken was repatriated to the U.S. with jaundice, weighing 112 pounds. He was hospitalized for eighteen of the next twenty-eight months, and his wife, Anita, visited every day.

After recovering, Ken went on to a very successful career in the entertainment industry. He was one of the first employees of Mercury Records and became their vice president of marketing. In 1966, he moved from Chicago to Los Angeles, where he was responsible for corporate development of the music division at Paramount and, later, MGM. "I loved my work, and I don't think that stress was ever really a problem for me. I was really dedicated. I hear people say that they work sixty hours a week and I think, 'So what?' It's not a big deal if you love what you're doing."

But health problems would continue to plague him. Ken had two heart attacks, followed by a double bypass operation in 1971. Four years later, he had a third heart attack. Since then he has survived prostate cancer, chronic obstructive pulmonary disease, arthritis, a gall bladder removal, hernias, and a second bypass operation. "I smoked for thirty-five years, and I know that played a role in my heart disease and pulmonary problems. Back in those days smoking was sophisticated. In the movies, Humphrey Bogart and Bette Davis smoked. Everybody smoked! When the Surgeon General's report came out in 1964 I decided to quit; but I gained eighteen pounds, and I couldn't fit into my suits anymore. So I went back to smoking. I even smoked after my first bypass operation. I finally quit for good after my third heart attack in 1975."

When Ken had his bypass operation in 1971, it was one of the first such operations performed in California. The doctors were unsure about the prognosis and advised Ken that he might only live for another five years. He worked for four years and then retired, unsure of what the future would hold.

"When I was working I never had a lot of time with my kids.

When they were little, sometimes I would get home after they were in bed. But after I retired I had a lot of time. That's one thing about retiring. You have a lot of time, and you've got to have something to do. If you love building things, buy a book about how to do it. I learned how to build. I learned how to wire. I learned how to plumb. I bought houses for each of my kids. I had more fun rebuilding kitchens, putting in new ovens, putting in new flooring, putting in new bathrooms. I got excited about putting in sprinkler systems and building a fence. It was just wonderful. I got back into their lives."

Ken has strong feelings about how he has survived so many physical problems. "I like life. I like being above ground, as they say. If you don't breathe, nothing else matters! And I think having a young attitude has a lot to do with it. I hate negativity. I look at life as a series of episodes. I don't expect to die; I expect to live with whatever I've got. And I have this belief that if something is 'broke,' then fix it. Thank God for the medicines today. There is so much they can fix. If you've got a problem then face it, solve it, and move on. That's the way I run my life.

"The other thing is that Anita has always been there for me, just as I have been there for her. I wouldn't say that she acts as a nurse, but it is always comforting to know that she is there. After sixty-one years together, we have some pretty strong feelings. I keep threatening her, 'I'm going to go before you do, so don't you dare check out on me.' We try to have fun with it, but we both realize that someday one of us is going to be very, very lonely. And I think that adds to our devotion now. I appreciate every day that I have her, and she feels the same. So we live for each other. We say a toast to each other at dinner every night, and when we go to sleep and when we get up we have a few words that we say about each other. It feels great, and I think it's healthy.

"I also think it is important to be focused on today. I don't really like to look back because the only thing that matters is what is happening right now. I've got stuff to do now. Why else would I be here?

"When I first retired, I had my workshop. That was my major focus for many years. I made all kinds of stuff for Anita and the boys. And I had fun doing that. I was also involved in some community activities and spent a lot of time with our grandsons. But they are older now and have their own activities. And now we are slowing down. It seems like there is some kind of mark once you hit eighty. But even then you have to keep focused on something. You always have to have something that you like to do. When life changes, you change with it."

During their lives, Jim Neher, Mary Ide, and Ken Myers have faced and overcome serious health issues. There is no way to know for certain whether Jim could have prevented his stroke by controlling his weight and blood pressure, whether Mary could have avoided her debilitating mobility problems with an exercise regimen, or whether Ken could have staved off the heart attacks and pulmonary problems by not smoking. What we do know, however, is that each of them could have significantly reduced the risk of those physical problems by changing their lifestyles.

Miriam Sims – *Healthy Choices*

MIRIAM SIMS GREW UP IN AUSTIN and graduated from the University of Texas with a bachelor's degree in Spanish and a master's in social work. After deciding she didn't want to spend the rest of her life as a counselor, she went back to get an MBA.

In the early 1980s, she founded Health Promotion Management, Inc., a firm that provides wellness programs to government agencies and private employers. "I started my business twenty years ago and sold it earlier this year. We have four full-time employees and a core group of twelve consultants who make presentations to our clients and their employees. It has been a great, fun business. Employees love it because it's a benefit to them. Our programs are designed to improve their mental and physical health and help them live better lives. And management likes it because it has the potential for cutting health care costs. It's also a pretty cost-effective way to tell their employees that management cares about them. So it really is a win-win thing. It has been wonderful work. When it was time for me to retire, I wasn't burned out, and I didn't want to totally quit. So, I negotiated to work half-time for three years."

The basic concept behind wellness is that we can all take actions to improve our health. As Miriam pointed out, the amount of control we have over our well-being is startling. "The MacArthur Foundation conducted a long-term, multidisciplinary research program designed to find out how older Americans could improve their physical and mental abilities. It was a series of studies, and their principal findings were that about seventy percent of how we age physically is actually under our control, and about fifty percent of how we age mentally is under our control. The genetic factor is not nearly as important as it was believed to be just ten years ago. And the importance of genetic inheritance declines the older we get. We can't control all illnesses, but in many cases our health is pretty much up to us.

"That concept of control is the foundation of our business. We succeed when we help people modify their behavior. Wellness is a process of being aware of and actively working toward better health. The keys are awareness and action. First, people need to have an understanding of their current health status. We help them by doing health screenings. Then, they have to take actions to improve their health. No matter where you are on the health continuum, you can move away from premature death and toward improved health. Wellness is a concept that applies to everybody.

"The wellness movement is really needed in our society.

Everyone knows that Americans are not doing enough to take care of themselves. Sixty percent of us are overweight. We eat too much, and we eat the wrong things. We don't exercise. Studies have shown that the best way to lose weight is to increase exercise. But even though ninety percent of Americans agree that exercise is an important part of healthy living, only fifteen percent of us get as much exercise as we should. And our lack of exercise hurts us mentally as well as physically because physical activity helps stimulate brain activity. Smoking is even worse. A Harvard Alumni Study found that the chance of people who smoke getting a heart attack is seven times greater than for people who don't.

"One book that has been around for a while but still does a good job of capturing what we talk about in many of our programs is *RealAge: Are You as Young as You Can Be?* by Dr. Michael Roizen. In the book, Dr. Roizen points out that some people are older than their chronological age and others are younger. The difference is how they live their lives. He discusses forty-four things that people can do to improve their health and reduce their 'RealAge.' Many of the things he talks about are very easy to do, but they can make a huge difference in people's lives.

"As Dr. Roizen observes, every little bit of physical activity helps. The more active you are, the younger you are. The more you exercise, the more calories you will burn, even when you're sitting still. Exercise affects everything—your cardiovascular system, your immune system, your muscular and skeletal systems, and your emotional well-being. This does not mean that you should overdo it. Forget the old line, 'No pain, no gain.' Exercise should not be painful. Pain is our body's way of telling us to back off.

"I also think it's important to challenge your brain and learn new things. We each have to find out what is interesting to us and then pursue it. I have read a lot of books about the brain and how to keep it active and functioning well. Stimulation is very important. When I sold my business, I wanted to keep working so that I would stay engaged. Crossword puzzles are great for a lot of people, but they just don't interest me. And I'm not good at them. Instead of that, every year I work at maintaining my Spanish skills. That's a challenge I am interested in. I guess the important thing is that everyone has to find mental stimulation by getting involved in something they really enjoy."

Stress management is also vitally important to health. Stress most often comes from factors beyond our control. "We try to teach people how to protect themselves from things that are out of their control. We talk about the control continuum. If you have no control, you just have to let it go. When you do have control, you should use it. Everything we talk about is in terms of positive health and taking charge where possible."

"There are so many things that we can do to improve the quality of our lives and our longevity. Take an aspirin a day. Supplement our diets with the right vitamins. Eat a balanced diet. Drink in moderation. Put on sunscreen. Walk. Get enough sleep. These are not that difficult, and they can have a tremendous impact on our lives and our longevity. Some actions are harder to take, like controlling our weight and blood pressure, stopping smoking, or learning how to manage stress. But people who are able to do these things can add many quality years to their lives. The message is that we can each have a huge impact on our success or failure in aging.

"Wellness is also about balance. It's about taking care of yourself and balancing your work life, your social life, your family life, and your spiritual life. The people who learn how to do that reap tremendous benefits." No one understands this better than Zalman Schachter-Shalomi.

Zalman Schachter-Shalomi – *Sage Advice*

RABBI ZALMAN SCHACHTER-SHALOMI has lived his life on the frontier, if not on the edge. He was born in Poland in 1924 and studied in Vienna. Under threat by the Nazis, his family moved to Antwerp and, later, was detained in Vichy, France. They escaped to Africa, sailed to the West Indies, and finally arrived in New York in 1941. Zalman studied at a Jewish seminary in Brooklyn and became a rabbi in 1947. Among other things, he has served as a teacher, congregational rabbi, campus chaplain, and professor of religion at Temple University in Philadelphia.

"Having been saved from the Holocaust, and since the leadership of our people had been decimated, I felt a need to give something back." He has. Reb Zalman is widely recognized as one of the most important Jewish spiritual teachers in the last fifty years. He is the author of over 150 articles and monographs on Jewish spiritual life and has translated many Hassidic and Kabbalistic texts. As chairman of Aleph, an alliance for Jewish renewal, he has worked tirelessly in a pioneering movement to renew Jewish spirituality in the contemporary world. To broaden his perspective, he studied with Sufi and Buddhist teachers, Native American elders, Catholic monks, and both humanistic and transpersonal psychologists. His approach has been to integrate the humanist insights of contemporary society with historical Jewish traditions, while emphasizing experience over doctrine.

As he approached his sixtieth birthday, Reb Zalman realized he was growing older and was feeling increasingly vulnerable. He began thinking about how he could convert his elder years into a blessing rather than a curse. After a forty-day retreat at an ecumenical center, he returned to work with renewed energy and a new vision that would transform his life and the lives of many who would follow his lead. In 1989, Reb Zalman founded the transdenominational Spiritual Eldering Institute, which

Sageing

sponsors seminars to help people realize their potential in their elder years. Since then, he has written four books: *Spiritual Intimacy* (1991), *Paradigm Shift* (1993), *Gate to the Heart* (1993), and *From Age-ing to Sage-ing* (1995) (co-authored with Ronald S. Miller).

"Most of us have grown up with a deep-seated fear and loathing of old age. Our youth-oriented culture, while touting aerobically perfect bodies and lifestyles, focuses obsessively on the physical diminishments associated with old age. Old age means wrinkled skin and chronic disease, rather than the wisdom, serenity, balanced judgment, and self-knowledge that represent the fruit of a long life experience. But the senior boom, with its interest in healthy lifestyle practices, lifelong learning, and political activism is helping to reverse the demeaning stereotypes that give old age a bad name. We are beginning to apply the insights of humanistic and transpersonal psychology and contemplative techniques from our spiritual tradition to the aging process itself."

Reb Zalman calls his model of late-life development "sage-ing." It is "a process that enables older people to become spiritually radiant, physically vital, and socially responsible 'elders of the tribe.'" Instead of passively succumbing to the diminishments of old age, elders become sages who continue to develop internally and who impart their inner knowledge, wisdom, judgment, and expanded consciousness to their children and other members of succeeding generations. Thus, sage-ing is the vehicle through which we continue personal development. At the same time, we are giving new relevance to our lives through the contributions we make to the welfare of society.

"People don't automatically become sages simply by living to a great age. They need to undertake the inner work that leads to expanded consciousness. They need to develop their contemplative skills. By doing so, they refute the notion that older people are closed-minded, set in their ways, and slow." And by passing

along the wisdom they gain through meditation and contem-
plation, they extend their productive years. "As long as we define
production as producing goods, we can say that older people are
less productive because they do slow down. But once we recognize that production can also be supplying services and mind
products we get a different perspective. There is a lot of that
going on."

According to Reb Zalman, not everyone has the potential to
become a sage. "The boomers need more awareness on how to
handle these life issues. And there are some people who grew up
during the Depression and knew only one thing all their lives—
nose to the grindstone, shoulder to the wheel, and produce for
their families. Now they can't do that anymore, but they never
raised their ceiling to look beyond what they have known. That
is very hard. Some of these people can't be helped because the
fear of what is ahead for them is so great. They are in a box. They
can't look to the future; they see only death. They can't look to
the past; they see only failure. And when they look at the present, they feel so diminished that they are in a psychic space like
Alzheimer's."

Reb Zalman has strong ideas about dealing with the inevitability of physical deterioration. "As we get older, we do not
have the same stamina and vigor that we had before. We have to
come to terms with the diminishment of our eyesight, hearing,
and so on. In *The Five Ages of Man*, Gerald F. Heard talks about
'involutional melancholia'—the depression that will come with
the deterioration of physiological functioning as we age if we
don't expect the changes and don't know how to deal with them.
To avoid this depression, you have to do that inner work to shift
the matrix of your awareness. You take advantage of the opportunity by understanding that this is a time in your life when you
can do something else in a more sedentary fashion. By doing the
contemplative work and by becoming involved in mentoring,
writing, journaling, and taking the distillate of life's experience

and saving it for the next generation, you will have a new reason to live and more to look forward to. You will experience a renewal.

"Let me also talk about coming to terms with mortality. When I last had an operation, I got wheeled into the operating room on a gurney. My sense was not that I had come to terms with *mortality*; it was that I had come to terms with *dying*. And that had such an impact on me. Up until then I said, 'Of course I am going to die someday.' But that did not seem real. Facing death is an emotional reality.

"People who do face death live out their days with greater zest and joy. Why is this so? As we age, we receive a number of messages about our mortality. We may be aware of shortened breath in climbing a steep grade or the need for longer recuperation time after an illness. In our society, we tend to mobilize our psychological defenses to tune these messages out, to deny the aging process. And over the years, we spend more and more energy to keep these reminders of our mortality at arm's length. But, as David Feinstein says in the *Rituals for Living and Dying*, 'When we confront our mortality, a shift occurs in our attention that makes us more aware of how precious life really is. We have an enhanced ability to accept ourselves, along with a greater ability to love. We lose the pervasive anxiety that makes us grasp obsessively for power, wealth, and fame. As we discover a deepened sense of purpose and a profound connectedness with other people, we tend to be motivated by higher, more universal values, such as love, beauty, truth, and justice.' (David Feinstein & Peg Elliot Mayo, *Rituals for Living and Dying: From Life's Wounds to Spiritual Awakening* [New York: Harper Collins, 1990])

"I also like what Ram Dass says about making peace with our mortality. He points out that our fear of death stems from a sense of separation from the whole of life. Our zeal for individuality has left us alienated not only from our families and communities, but from nature and its commonwealth of species. What gives aging its intuitive meaning, he says, is a sense of oneness with Earth's life cycles, the procession of the seasons and the alternating rhythms of birth, growth, decay, death, and transformation into new life. When we are shielded from these awesome mysteries, we identify with our separateness and come to fear death. But once we recognize that we are part of the whole, our fear of death dissipates immensely.

"The shows that people see on television, like *ER*, are based on the notions that death is horrible and violent, and that we have to save life at any cost. When people do die, they are placed under a white sheet, and there is a conspiracy of silence about it. Imagine, instead, a more positive image of death. There is a beautiful deathbed. The person who is dying is thankful for his good life, fulfilled by what he has accomplished, and prepared to let go. He is content that his children are taking over and considers it to have been a privilege to have the opportunity of life. The message is totally different. Being present to a good death helps a lot. So, we need to create a different atmosphere about death. Rather than the atmosphere of fear, we need to understand that death is inevitable, and a good death is a wonderful thing.

"Hospice does a good job in many respects, but Hospice education can be improved. The concentration is on palliative care, on how to make death easy and not painful—and on how to help the grieving families. But there isn't the effort to accompany a person into their death place. That they haven't learned yet.

"Woody Allen says, 'Death is not a bad thing. I just don't want to be there.' Well, how could you not want to be there? Your life flashes before you. There is a sense of peacefulness and a floating sensation. It's such a moment! So I tell people, 'Prepare for that. What music would you like to hear? Who would you like to have around your deathbed? And who would you not like to have around your deathbed?' I think that this makes a difference. You should say to yourself, 'Well, it's going to happen to me anyway, so how can I make this a pleasant thing?'

"Ten years ago I took a hang-glider ride. Everything in my experience told me that I shouldn't do it, that it was crazy. But then there was the *feeling* of how the air was holding me up, that there was nothing underneath. After a while I was thinking ... WHEE! I am flying like Superman. Those were the most wonderful fifteen minutes I have had in my life. Now when friends visit me, I take them to the airport for a glider ride. It is like a preparation for when the soul is out of the body."

Observations about Managing Health

RETIREMENT IS A REALITY CHECK. When we retire, we should develop a new concept of time. It is no longer boundless, as it was when we were younger. If we are lucky, we may have ten years of good health remaining. If we are really lucky, we may have twenty. We may, however, only have an hour and a half. In any event, retirement is the time to acknowledge that change is inevitable and to act accordingly.

Our first step should be to take actions to improve our health and, quite possibly, our longevity as well. It is well documented that the leading causes of death in the U.S. are heart attacks, cancer, and strokes. Together, they account for more than sixty percent of the deaths in the country each year. But according to Partnership for Prevention, the leading cause of premature death is poor behavioral patterns. The Harvard Center for Cancer Prevention states that fifty percent of all cancer in the U.S. could be avoided—or at the very least delayed—by controlling weight, eliminating tobacco use, eating healthy diets, exercising, and decreasing alcohol use. The American Heart Association concurs and adds that those actions, along with controlling blood pressure, cholesterol, and diabetes, would substantially reduce the number of heart attacks and strokes. Thus, the principal reason that there are *so many* cases of heart

attacks, cancer, and strokes is that a lot of people make bad decisions. It is really more accurate to say that the leading causes of
death in America are poor choices and lack of discipline.

While we are taking actions to improve our physical health,
we should also attend to our mental health and acuity. Obviously, exercise and proper diets are important. Exercise is even
an integral part of the training for master chess players. But
regular mental stimulation that challenges us is even more
imperative. In fact, research has shown that stimulating the
mind helps ward off Alzheimer's disease and other forms of
dementia. We should identify challenging mental activities that
we enjoy and pursue them regularly to stimulate our brains.
Another way to remain stimulated is to stay actively engaged
with other people. Social involvement and the ability to develop
new friends are among the predictors of good cognitive and
intellectual functioning during retirement. As we age, friends
will move away or die. If we don't develop new friendships, our
social worlds may shrink.

We can also improve our health by adopting and maintaining
positive attitudes. As discussed in Chapter One, positive attitudes are a common denominator for people who find happiness and fulfillment in retirement. And optimism plays a
particularly important role in health maintenance. In his 1988
best seller, *Learned Optimism*, Martin Seligman observes that
pessimism produces inertia, is a self-fulfilling prophecy, makes
people feel bad, is associated with poor health, and promotes
depression. He even concludes that in many cases depression is
just an extreme form of pessimism. By contrast, optimists have
better health habits and better immune systems, get fewer
infections, and live longer. Medical research in the intervening
years has confirmed and expanded on these conclusions. We
now know that optimists deal more effectively with stress, have
better lung function, and are better able to cope with health

challenges. They also feel healthier, which is the most important factor in improving life satisfaction. No wonder optimists live longer, happier lives!

Optimism works because, like pessimism, it is a self-fulfilling prophecy. But while pessimists think that they are at the mercy of the future, optimists believe that they can change it. As a result, optimists take actions that may bring about favorable results.

However, optimism can bring positive results even in the absence of specific actions. Anecdotal evidence has shown that belief, faith, and confidence are powerful drivers. In some cases, placebos are as effective as dedicated medical treatments, and primitive medicine men have cured illnesses even though their methods have no pharmacological efficacy. In other words, our health is directly affected by our mindset and expectations.

The comments from the people in the Retirement Puzzle Cohort are consistent with these findings. In particular, Jim, Mary, and Ken all mentioned that they believe their positive attitudes played significant roles in helping them overcome their physical setbacks. For most of us attitude is a choice. If we choose to do so, we can make a tremendous difference in our own lives.

Not everyone is so fortunate. Some are born with genetic conditions that portend unfortunate physical or mental outcomes. Others acquire diseases or experience accidents that prevent them from guiding their own destiny. Even for those with a natural tendency toward optimism, the challenge to remain optimistic becomes greater with age. But as Nancy, Miriam, and most health professionals know, it is worth the continued effort because optimism will positively affect our physical and mental well-being.

Once we have addressed the issue of improving our health, we need to change hats. We all want to live healthy, full lives as long as providence allows, but we know that physical decline and mortality are inevitable. And the game clock is ticking.

If we fail to recognize the inevitability of deteriorating health, we may suffer the consequences of the "involutional melancholia" that Reb Zalman mentioned. But facing reality seems more prudent than subjecting ourselves to the likelihood of depression. Facing reality will also help us to plan more properly for the future and will enable us to make crucial decisions about issues such as long-term care insurance and long-term living arrangements. Addressing these issues early rather than later will be a service to our kids and to ourselves.

Finally, it is increasingly apparent that coming to terms with mortality can improve the quality of our life experiences. In *Tuesdays with Morrie*, Mitch Albom quotes a dying Morrie Schwartz as saying, "Everyone knows they're going to die, but nobody believes it. If we did, we would do things differently" and, "Once you learn how to die, you learn how to live." We know that people who have had life-threatening experiences often reevaluate their values and interests. As Jim Neher and Reb Zalman observe, these people see life in a new light. They experience an awakening. Some even comment that, having survived, they would never trade the experience. For them, the threat of death gave life renewed meaning, a poignancy previously missing.

By addressing our mortality, we come to recognize how we fit into our world. And by reaching out to contribute to our loved ones and our society, we enhance our lives and find meaning and purpose during our retirement years. The inner work, described by Reb Zalman, should occur throughout our lives. But it becomes increasingly important as we make the transition from the first or active phase of our retirement into the second, more passive phase. What a wonderful time to embrace a new challenge!

THE FOURTH CHALLENGE:
Revitalizing Relationships

(It's about family, friends, and legacies.)

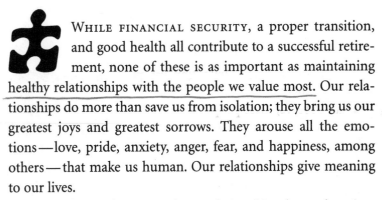 WHILE FINANCIAL SECURITY, a proper transition, and good health all contribute to a successful retirement, none of these is as important as maintaining healthy relationships with the people we value most. Our relationships do more than save us from isolation; they bring us our greatest joys and greatest sorrows. They arouse all the emotions—love, pride, anxiety, anger, fear, and happiness, among others—that make us human. Our relationships give meaning to our lives.

In retirement, however, these relationships keep changing. And we have to respond appropriately. Entering retirement, spouses need to adapt to a new lifestyle together, and as they age they will experience other changes as well. Some of our kids will marry and have children of their own, altering our relationships with them and creating new bonds with grandchildren. Relationships with friends will also change, as old friends move out of our lives and new friendships develop. While this is important to everyone, it is particularly important for those who are not involved in long-term relationships.

Adapting to these changes is essential, because research shows that the ability to maintain existing relationships and develop new friendships is a reliable predictor of life satisfaction in retirement. Moreover, the contributions we make to our partners, families and friends—the way in which we positively touch their lives—may well be our most important legacy.

Changing relationships demand increased sensitivities. We must learn how to revitalize our relationships, to keep them fresh and alive. In this chapter, we meet four people who have gained important insights into how this can be accomplished. We also receive advice from an acclaimed marriage and family therapist who has dedicated his career to helping people develop healthier relationships and improve their lives.

Mary Elliott –
Making Marriages Work in Retirement

MARY ELLIOTT and her husband, Bob, are soul mates. Sweethearts since attending Catholic high schools, they married and raised four kids. They have shared the same lifelong friends and enjoyed the same recreational activities. Together they have endured major family health problems and the death of one daughter. During the twenty years after their youngest child graduated from high school, Mary managed the front office of Bob's dental practice.

"I was able to stay at home to raise the kids when they were growing up. But when they were grown, I helped Bob out at the office. So we were together during the days, and our experience was a lot different from most other couples. Our kids used to ask me, 'How do you do it? How can you be together all day long and then again at night?' But part of it was that he was in charge at the office and I took more responsibility at home. That was one hard thing about the change into retirement. It was difficult for him to leave his office and patients, and it was hard for me to let him in here at home. But you both have to do it. You have to figure out how to make it work. I know that it is a lot tougher for other people than it was for us, because we had worked together all of those years and the change was not so dramatic.

"During the first six months after we stopped working, the change in our daily routines was a little bit of an issue. Our lives were no longer structured around work. So maybe there were some awkward moments, but it worked itself out. We've been together long enough that it wasn't a big problem for us. I do know that there are some women who have had that problem. I guess each couple has to figure out what will work for them.

"From talking to my friends, I have learned that when men who have really been work-oriented leave their jobs and start spending a lot more time around the home, they often end up wanting to be a bigger part of their wives' lives. A lot of women have a problem with that. When husbands constantly ask, 'Where have you been?' or 'Where are you going?' or 'Who was that on the phone?' it is like an invasion of their privacy. These women have led their own lives all of their adult years, and now that someone is constantly checking up on them, it creates pressure. Listening to my friends, this seems to be a bigger source of stress in retirement than anything else. Men need to have their own friendships and activities to keep their interest so they are not totally dependent on their wives. Most women I know encourage their husbands to get involved with other people and other activities so that they both have some independence.

"Women need to have time to ourselves, whether it is to go shopping or go out and be with our women friends. We need some time to be in our homes alone, to have some privacy. One of the advantages of retirement is that you have more time to share things together, but you can't do it full-time or you'll drive each other crazy. Everybody needs at least some independence, and husbands and wives have to figure out how to make that happen. It's not always easy.

"Bob and I haven't taken separate vacations, but there have been times when we've been apart for a while. I don't always join him when he goes hunting, and I have gone back to be with my family alone. I think that being apart every once in a while is a good thing. It is good to have some time apart during the day, and it can also be helpful to have some time apart during the year. Breaks like that help reenergize us and make the time we are together that much better."

Mary believes that many different factors contribute to a happy marriage in retirement. "Two of the keys are communication and patience. The couples who did not communicate well before they retired probably won't do it after they retire. But if they want to be happy together, they are going to have to learn how to communicate effectively. You can't be happy spending as much time together as you do in retirement and not communicate.

"Patience is also important. When you retire, little things can become big things. If you're not careful, you can drive each other crazy with irritating habits — like telling the same stories over and over — especially because you are together more. Part of the problem may just be getting older. When we were younger, there was so much going on in our lives that we didn't have time to let the little things irritate us. But now that we're older and there is less going on, the little things can grow. People need to be aware of that. You can't let little issues become big issues. You have to keep everything in perspective.

"You also need to be flexible. Each person in a marriage must take responsibility for certain things. You each know the other's limitations. You know when your spouse won't do something.

Rather than complaining about it, it is often better to just take charge and do it yourself. After you retire you have the time, and it will make your lives together that much better. So why end up arguing about something that really doesn't matter? It makes more sense to pick your issues and stand up when something is really important to you.

"Another key to being happy as a couple in retirement is to be realistic. I think everyone should be goal-oriented. But some people set goals that are not attainable, and then they are disappointed. So I think being realistic is crucial. You have to be on the same page.

"Lately, one of our issues has been whether or not we should move. It's not a big concern, but we haven't resolved it yet either. I would like to be in a smaller house, but Bob likes this neighborhood and the thought of moving all of our stuff is more than he wants to tackle. I don't know what we'll do, but we'll keep on talking about it until we figure it out. Moving to be nearer our kids is not really the issue. They are all married, and they have their own lives. And that's the way it should be.

"We try not to over-involve ourselves with our grandkids, but when we are with them we are really focused. We do what the grandkids want to do. We're there strictly for them. But we have the same concerns that a lot of our friends have with their kids and grandkids. Our idea of parenting is different from that of our kids. We aren't as liberal. We think their kids have too much stuff, and we think as parents our kids should be more consistent in disciplining the grandkids. But we also know what our roles are now. So we try not to overstep our bounds."

Mary's comments reaffirm what most of us already know. The keys to a successful marriage in retirement are the same keys to a successful marriage before retirement: trust and love. "There is no perfect marriage, and there has to be some luck involved for things to go as well as they have for us. We have faced a lot of challenges during our marriage, but we have survived because we have had each other to rely on. I think that good marriages are based on being there for each other and trusting each other. Some of the most meaningful communication is non-verbal. You have to know that you can count on each other. Having money and having your health are both important, but nothing is as important as having relationships with people you love and who love you back."

Leslie Hamilton – *Going It Alone*

LESLIE HAMILTON LEARNED HOW TO TAKE CHARGE early in life. On a summer day when she was fifteen, her parents had an argument. A few hours later, her dad had a heart attack and died. He was forty-one. At the funeral, some people pulled her aside and told her that she would have to take care of her mother and younger brother because she was the "strong one." In the ensuing years, Leslie tried hard to comfort her mother who was absorbed by a debilitating guilt.

Leslie married when she was twenty-one but divorced her husband nine years later—after one daughter and more exasperation with her needy husband than she was willing to tolerate. She became a middle-level English teacher and raised her daughter alone. Now in her late fifties, Leslie is retired. Over the years, she has had some relationships, but independence has always won out over commitment. The heart-breaking experiences of her earlier years may explain why.

Leslie's thoughts about her father's death are introspective. "It was probably my most defining moment. Death is so awful. It creates such tragedy and sadness. But when it happens to one of your parents during your teenage years, it can also bring a rebirth—a definition of who you are going to become. For me, that sadness created a sense of aloneness and independence.

I have often looked back on my life and realized that I could have become an emotional mess. I've wondered how I was able to choose a path of strength and independence instead.

"I was one of the very first people to have a subscription to *Ms. Magazine* and I coveted those *Ms.* issues for years. They helped open my eyes to who I could become. And I changed, not only because of the awakening of the women's movement, but also because of the drain caused by my relationship with my ex-husband.

"I have had other relationships, but I see myself as an independent woman who is going it alone. I have always been fairly comfortable with this because I have been that way since an early age. I ask myself, 'If not for me, who is going to do it? Who is going to get things done?' And I have just accepted the challenge. But even though this is a strength, there is a weakness inside too. It's a dichotomous kind of thing. I want to be strong and I want the challenges, but inside there are also times when I think it would be nice to have somebody take care of me.

"Early on I struggled with my confidence, even though I was a cheerleader and class officer. Even though I was always in front of people, I sort of feigned confidence. I worried about what other people thought. And I sure don't think I was alone in that. I think everybody has experienced it. But with age comes the freedom to be ourselves. Now I think, 'If they love me, they love me. If they don't, they don't. So be it.'"

Since she retired from teaching, Leslie has been active. "I really fill my days. I am constantly on the go with friends and groups. That is the way I find some happiness. I have my school group that meets for lunch and does other activities. I walk, practice yoga, and spend a lot of time talking with my friends. They are such an important part of my life. I have an interest in numerology. I have redecorated my house and helped some friends do some decorating. I was never able to read as much as

I do now. I also travel a lot. Since retirement, I have gone on three significant world adventures with friends. And I have noticed that in the last three years I have been branching out to younger people. But I still rely mostly on my older, established relationships.

"I am secure with who I am and what I am doing right now, but I am always searching for new things to catch my interest. I'm okay, and I always seem to have enough to do. But I am looking ahead. And I am watching what others are doing.

"I'm not scared of growing old; I just want to have a plan. And I know that if I don't make one, nobody else is going to do it for me. I have always made lists, and in the first few months of retirement I discovered that if I didn't make a list of what I was going to do, I would flounder a little bit. So make a list, even if you don't do everything on it. Just having certain goals has really helped me.

"Being alone can lead to melancholy—sort of a cloud hanging over me. I never quite know when it is going to come. I know this may sound simplistic, but what helps me is that I just let it wash over me. I go to the park and do a lot of walking. Nature is the best rejuvenator for me, the best medicine. It is different from being with my girlfriends because being in nature allows me to tap into my innermost being. When I am alone with nature, I can totally be myself.

"But I have had some strange feelings in the last six months to a year. Most of my really good friends are married, and they have wonderful marriages. So I have felt a little bit of a longing. I wonder what it would be like. Could I ever have that? Would I want to change? And I ask myself, 'Why am I having those feelings now?' I think it is partly because I have much more time by myself than I did when I was working. But I don't make any attempts to change anything.

"Another thing that really is tough for single people—

especially for single women with children—is the money issue. It has always plagued me, and it has plagued a very good friend of mine who is in a similar situation. We have always talked about how clever we are in figuring out how to make it, being on the edge and watching the checkbook at the end of every month. A single woman has more financial issues than a single male. I had no help from my ex-husband with my daughter's college education. So she and I both had school loans when she graduated.

"We are very, very close, and now that she has children, I travel to be with them several times a year. It gets expensive, but somehow I do it. I figure it out. And, yet, I still worry every single month. So money is the biggest stressor I have in my life. It is the main thing that will put me into that funk where I need to go take my nature walks.

"I have, as I think every retired single person does, more worries than great expectations for the future. I wonder about what is going to happen. We only have so many years left on this planet, and sometimes I wonder if my life would be better during that time if I had a companion. But I have been so independent for so long that I don't *have* to be in a relationship. I don't *need* companionship at the end of the day. I have done okay for so many years that I trust myself to be okay in the future. I know deep down who I am, and I couldn't be in a relationship unless there was mutual respect. There are many men who expect respect but have trouble returning it. You'd better just live the best life that you can live in this moment. I think the secret is that you can't become too full of yourself. Just be a flexible optimist and roll with life as it comes to you."

Jo Kearney – *Getting Your Priorities Straight*

JO KEARNEY HAS AN INFECTIOUS SMILE that lights up a room. She exudes happiness and shares it with everyone around her.

After raising four girls and a boy, Jo became a very successful real estate broker. Her business philosophy mimics her personal philosophy — show that you care for others and everything else will fall into place.

"I really tried to be of service to people. I never thought about the commissions. I've always wanted to help others. Whether it was the tiniest little condominium or a multi-million dollar house, it really didn't matter to me. I always wanted to be of service. It is really a joy to find somebody a home or to sell their home and help them solve a problem. People appreciate that, and I think it probably shows. If you show you care about others, the money will come."

Despite her success in real estate, it is far from her first love. Early on, Jo learned what was important to her. "When I was in college and started thinking about what I wanted to do with my life, I tried to visualize what would make me the happiest. And the image that came was of me in a kitchen with a bunch of little kids dyeing Easter eggs. It was an incredibly happy scene and I was dressed perfectly and the kitchen was immaculate. That is how I learned that I wanted to have a large family and be at the center of joyful children."

Jo met her future husband, John, who had similar family goals. Not surprisingly, their first daughter was born eleven months after they married. The moment still resonates. "One thing I know for sure is that from the minute you hold your first-born in your arms until your last breath, you are a mother. It never, ever leaves you. It is the greatest joy in the world. Your heart goes up and down with your children. You are with them forever. And it's just wonderful!

"When they are little, you are their nurturer and teacher. You are the chief operating officer, feeding them, getting them to their lessons, helping them with their homework, and keeping them safe. Then you go through a period when you can't be with them all the time and you pray a lot that everything you taught them, the values and everything else, will keep them safe. If you have been fortunate, like we have been, when they reach adulthood your children turn out to be your best friends. That has just been the greatest joy of John's and my lives. Our kids have been our biggest priority since the day they were born—and they still are.

"Our main goal in raising kids to adulthood—and going through their ups and downs—was to help empower them to do the right thing on their own. But even though they are now adults, I will drop everything in five minutes and run to be with my kids when they need me. And I'll always continue to do that. The main thing we can give our kids is the knowledge that we love them unconditionally and that we will be there for them. I don't think that there is anything more important than that.

"The hardest part of my life has been having a demanding job and a large family—and trying to be all things to all people. Keeping everything in balance has been challenging. But now with adult kids as my best friends, it is a joy to be their confidant. We talk all the time. It's mainly just sharing the days, but because of that constant communication I think that we are in on more of what is going on in their lives than many other parents. The most important things I have learned are to be a good listener, to not give advice unless it is asked for, to be a supporter and cheerleader, to respect their adulthood, and to be there when they need me. You have to remember what you went through to get to where you are in life. It was by learning. Sometimes that means going through difficult experiences. I have also learned to be a silent listener when they are upset with their spouses. Never agree with them, because tomorrow they will probably make up.

"There is joy in loving your kids unconditionally, but to do that you have to sacrifice. We have lovingly sacrificed, and that has become a reward in itself. As we grow older and become less selfish in terms of our own wants and needs, it is a powerful thing to refocus on our children and our children's children. The greatest thing for us as parents is to watch our family grow and develop. There is such joy that comes from moving beyond thinking about ourselves so that we can focus more on these wonderful people that we have become the stewards for. What greater blessing is there in life beyond being a steward for the people who mean so much to you?

"Since I have five children, people have asked me how I have room to love more than one or two. I can tell you, now with ten grandchildren, it is amazing how your heart expands so that you have room to fully love each person who comes into your life like that. When I held my first grandchild the day she was born, I was shocked by the power of the connection. It was a jolt. She was immediately part of me.

"In fact, I have been at the birth of six of my ten grandchildren, and I even helped deliver one of them in my daughter's living room. Talk about being close to your grandkids! Each one is totally unique. They are all gifts of joy. And there are some advantages to having grandchildren. You don't have the responsibility. You don't have to worry about getting up at two in the morning. You don't have to get up again at five. You don't have the challenges of raising them. But they are in your thoughts, and you do worry about them."

Like Mary Elliott, Jo has some concerns about the way children are being raised today. "There is a permissiveness now, and I think it is a huge disservice to the children. Children need to have reasonable parameters. They feel so secure when they know what their guidelines are. Sometimes you think that you would like to offer your opinions about how to raise children. But you have to respect your kids' adulthood, and they have to learn to do things on their own. In some cases, you may be able to show by example, but you can't impose. You have to respect their family unit. If you don't, you just breed ill will. This is probably the hardest part about having adult kids who are parents."

As important as Jo's family is to her, there is also a special place in her life for her friends. "If I didn't have the relationships that I have with my close friends, my life would be very unfulfilled. We trust each other. We rely on each other. When we are down, we share our thoughts. Because of them, I feel that I never have to carry a load by myself. If I need a hug, I can ask for it. If I want to share my joys, they will just be thrilled for me. I truly believe that my friends have been at the heart of my joy in life.

"Family members are great, but responsibilities always go hand in hand with them. So even though my husband and kids are my best friends, my other close friends add a whole different dimension to my life. They give me a carefree, joyous connection. There is camaraderie, trust, and a sharing of life's experiences without any expectations. Being with them is a total release from everything else that goes on in my life. In so many ways, life is fulfilling if you have a handful of friends you can trust. I feel sorry for the people who never experience that, because my friends just round out my life. I can't imagine what my life would be like without my girlfriends.

"Life is a series of ups and downs, peaks and valleys. If we can be a constant for the people in our lives through these cycles, just being there for them and providing our love and giving them positive support, we get so much in return. At this age, when we step back and think about what is important, it is not the jobs or money or things that are important. What is important is our family—and our friends."

Ken Pinson – *Friendships That Change Your Life*

KEN PINSON IS WELL TRAVELED. During the summers of his college years, he spent time in Canada, Europe, and Brazil. After graduating from the University of Texas in 1955, he became an

Air Force pilot. Since there were no civilian pilot jobs available when his tour of duty was over, he went to work for the Ford Motor Company. Over the next thirty years, his sales and marketing jobs at Ford required frequent moves. After retiring, he became a real estate investor and traveled extensively until he and his wife, Kathy, got tired of long airplane rides.

Since Kathy was a child psychologist, Ken decided to do some volunteer work at a mental health center and ultimately became a counselor for a group of senior men. It has been an eye-opening experience. Ken has learned a great deal about the importance of personal relationships — particularly after we retire.

"Moving to a new town after retirement can be a problem because you may not have any established friends. I have come to realize that friendships are really important when you are retired, because you don't have the built-in social interactions that you had while you were still working. I have always had a lot of acquaintances but not many close friends because we moved so often. People who have long-established close friends don't know how lucky they really are. They have a dimension to their lives that has been lacking in mine.

"Fortunately, I have a wonderful relationship with my wife. So my need for male bonding is probably not as great as it would be otherwise. But, it is still important. Having friends that I see during the day keeps me involved. Through them, I gain new experiences, and I also have more interesting things to talk about with my wife when we come together at the end of the day.

"When I look back, my four years in college were probably the most stimulating and mind-expanding years of my life. The environment was great. I was surrounded by people who were vibrant and motivated to learn. They were interested and interesting. But it seems that as people move into the workaday world, and later when they retire, they lose a lot of that intellectual curiosity. It also seems that adult men are reluctant to talk openly about their feelings. They will talk about facts and issues, but they are hesitant to really open up. If we could figure out how to recapture our intellectual curiosity and openness in retirement, it would be wonderful."

Ken admits to some complicity in this. "It is very difficult for me to encourage other people to share their deepest thoughts or problems. I am not good at asking leading questions because I feel like I am trespassing, invading other people's private space. I am more willing to open up my own feelings, but even there I am a bit reserved."

Nevertheless, he has enjoyed working with the group of senior men and feels that he is making a worthwhile contribution. "Through the Mental Health Center, I work with a group of men who are between their mid-seventies and early nineties. It started off as group therapy for men whose wives had died. But as the group evolved, we realized that these men really don't want to talk about their losses. At this point in their lives, they have suffered a lot. In addition to losing their wives, they have had physical losses. They don't see or hear or move like they used to. Some have had memory losses. One guy loved to ride his bike and can no longer do that. Some are no longer able to drive cars. The issue comes down to how we deal with the losses we experience as we age.

"What becomes clear is the need for relationships with other people. I don't know whether this group of men is representative of senior men overall, because several have recently moved to be near their families and don't have any other well-established relationships. So, their need for friendship is probably greater than it is for people who have lived in the community for a longer time. Some of these guys don't have any family members left. Others worry that they are a burden to their kids and are spending the money that they had hoped to leave for them. Some feel that their lives are now devoid of meaning. They are depressed, and I think their depression is probably the reason that they sought out our group.

"We provide a chance for them to be involved in meaningful conversation every week. But we have found that these guys don't want to talk about the things that are going on in the world, and they don't want to talk about their feelings. So, we just let the conversation go wherever it goes. And usually it goes to reminiscing. They love to talk about their military experiences and their work experiences. They like to talk about when they were younger, and they're a lot less interested in talking about what is going on today. They think they are beyond the point where they can control anything or influence what is going on. Since there is nothing that they can do about it, they don't see any reason to get even more depressed by talking about it.

"How do we deal with that? The challenge is to give these guys something to live for, to give some meaning to their lives. That is what we try to do. And what works? What works is getting them interested in each other. The thing that unites them is that they can understand and relate to one another. At least, that has been my experience.

"At first, they just enjoyed having an audience that would listen to their own reminiscing. But over time most of them have learned to become more group-centered. Most have become better listeners. They are more interested in what the other people have to say. I think that is the real message. When we listen to other people, when we begin to think about someone other than ourselves, when we show concern for something other than our own problems, we become more engaged. And that makes our own lives better."

Neil Rosenthal – *Why Relationships Matter*

NEIL ROSENTHAL IS A HIGHLY REGARDED marriage and family therapist who specializes in personal relationships — what goes wrong with them and what people can do to strengthen them. Neil's weekly newspaper column, "Relationships," is nationally and internationally syndicated. He has been listed in *The Directory of Distinguished Americans, Who's Who, Men of Achievement,* and *Who's Who of Emerging Leaders in America.*

Neil feels very strongly about the importance of relationships in retirement. "I think that retirement will be cruel to people who do not have intimate relationships. If they are not married or in committed, long-term relationships, if they don't have close connections with their children, parents, or friends, then they are in deep trouble. They are at risk. How many games of golf can you play, how many *Wheel of Fortune* and *I Love Lucy* reruns can you watch, before you feel like your life is empty and that you are approaching the end of your life without much to show for it? You can be the healthiest person in the world and have a beautiful house, a vacation villa, and a huge retirement account, but I don't think you will be happy.

"You need closeness in your life. I am talking about close, intimate people in your world. If you don't have that with your friends, with your lady or man, with your parents or your children, you are going to find that retirement is hell. You will go to hell in some metaphoric way. Most people who are alone feel empty and unfulfilled and purposeless. Even if you have a mission in your life, like writing a book or visiting all of the islands off the coast of Greece, life will have a feeling of incompleteness. You have to have fulfilling relationships in your life to avoid this emptiness. And the more connected and close your relationships are, the richer your life is going to be. If you don't have them, you're not going to feel good about your life no matter what else you have done. You will be missing the critical component. You will have failed to cultivate the essence of what it is to be human and the essence of what it is to feel happy."

Marriage by itself is not the answer. "Many people are married but do not have an intimate relationship. Many people!

They may live together. They may have a sexual relationship, but they are not close. They have spent thirty or forty or fifty years avoiding each other emotionally, avoiding the key issues of intimacy and closeness. So when they enter retirement, they're in the alarming position of being with each other 24/7 and not being close friends.

"We have the notion in our culture that sex is the most intimate thing we can do, but it's not. An intimate relationship is not about sex. The most intimate thing we can do is let someone else really know us. Let them in completely. An intimate relationship is one in which we have made an emotional investment. The other person *really* matters to us. We have strong, powerful feelings. And because of that we have become vulnerable. We are psychologically interdependent. Just the thought that something could go wrong with the person we care for is threatening. And if anything does go wrong for the other person or with the relationship, it shakes up our world."

Men and women both struggle to form intimate relationships. "Maybe women are better at forming casual friendships. But when you go to a deeper level, when you go to committed and intimate long-term relationships, women are no more competent than men at letting others into their inner worlds. Both are scared. The cultural myth is that women are good at this and men are bad at it. But that has not been my personal experience.

"There is one communication topic that we should talk about. If you are trying to improve the relationship with the man or the woman in your life, if you wake up and realize you are not as close as you want to be, it may be necessary to talk about things that you have ignored or have been taking for granted. Talk about what makes you happiest or most frustrated or makes you feel misunderstood. Be open with your partner. If we want closer relationships, we must be able to speak about our needs and our truths with each other. If we can't tell each other who we are and what we want and what we need, how can we feel closer?

"Another thing we should do is check in with each other every day. Ask, 'How are you doing? How are you feeling? Is there anything you would like from me?' This is just checking in, but it is really important. When you do that you are opening up. You are showing that you care and are inviting your partner to open up to you. You are showing that you value his or her happiness. And your partner will sense that and will feel he or she is special. Every man and every woman wants to feel special. But remember that if you invite the feedback, you'd better be willing to be receptive, because if you aren't you will be shooting yourself in the foot. You have to be sincere.

"Friendships are not the same as our primary intimate relationships. There are similarities, but there is not the same level of dependency and vulnerability. When we have friends, we judge them on different criteria than we use to judge a spouse or our parents or children. A friend can have irritating personal habits that you could never live with, but you're never going to have to live with them. Your friend can do things that you might roll your eyes at, but it doesn't make any difference. Friendships are about supporting each other. It's a different kind of relationship than we have when we live with someone like our parents, spouses, and children. All of these are intimate relationships, but friends are defined and judged differently. And those friendships are really important—especially if you don't have a primary intimate relationship. The more intimate relationships you have, the fuller your life is going to be.

"In an intimate primary relationship, we give our heart and soul and spirit. We share our hopes and wishes and dreams. We are open about our vulnerabilities, fears, and irritations. Our partners get so much more of us than our friends do, more of the good and more of the bad. With our friends, we role-play more. With our friends, we are more careful. This can be good. If everyone was as careful in their primary relationships as they are with their close friends, the world would be a better place. But when we go home, we feel permission to be ourselves. Frequently, that means that we let the worst of ourselves out."

How do we determine when it is appropriate to keep private thoughts to ourselves, and when we should talk about them? "I think you should draw the line if you are going to hurt your partner when it is not essential to do so. There is one commandment missing from the Ten Commandments: Thou shalt not commit intentional hurt. Isn't that what the Golden Rule means, 'Do unto others...?' I think you draw the line when you are causing intentional hurt. Why are you saying something? If you can't live with things the way they are, you *have* to say it. If there is a goal in mind that will improve the relationship, you *should* say it. But if there is no residual benefit and you are just being hurtful, you *shouldn't* say it.

"Frequently what passes as a communication problem is actually a failure to show that we value the other person — that we are happy they are in our lives and know we are better off because of it. Married people, people who have been together for years and years and years, people who should know better, become reluctant to reveal how important the other person is."

The problem often surfaces when couples retire and spend more time together. Neil recalled what happened when his uncle retired. "Shortly after he retired, I talked to my aunt. She said, 'He's in my house all the time. He's under foot. I don't know what to do with him.' I said, 'You've been married for forty years. He belongs there. He pays the mortgage.'

"But the real solution is that we have to have realms of interest together and we have to have our own separate realms of interest. We each have to have our own lives. Not that we are unwilling to share with our partners, but we each need our own sense of self. We each need to be able to do the things that are of interest to us and to respect our partners for doing the things that are interesting to them. I think most people feel more alive and vital when they have their own fulfilling experience during the day. And they have something to talk about at the end of the day, something that is more interesting than what happened on the daytime soaps. But we also should have things that we enjoy doing together. So we have our separate worlds and our joint worlds. Both are essential."

As important as Neil feels intimate relationships are, he agrees that they alone will not bring us fulfillment. "Intimate relationships are one key—but not the only key—to having a full life. Simply having intimate relationships is not enough. We need more in our lives. We need to have goals to shoot for. We need to have things to do. We need to feel productive. These can be whatever we choose, as long as they keep us motivated and involved."

Observations about Revitalizing Relationships

OVER THE YEARS, I have attended a few Berkshire Hathaway annual meetings chaired by Warren Buffett. Mr. Buffett, noted for being bright, thoughtful, and the most successful investor in the modern era, is reputedly the second wealthiest person in the world. At one meeting, he was asked to define "success." His response, as best I can recall it, was that he has known many high achievers who are thought to be successful. Some of them are happy and are enjoyable to be around, while others are miserable and have many people who hate them. He doesn't think that we should call the second group successful.

Buffett believes that we will be successful in life if the people who we hope to have love us *do* love us. He says that love is one thing that we can't get rid of. The more we try to give love away, the more we receive in return. So if we give love to other people throughout our lives, we will keep getting more back. By the end of our lives, there will be a huge reservoir of love. Buffett thinks that the love we give and the love we receive during our lives is probably the best measure of our success.

Interesting, isn't it? Warren Buffett's path to success and Neil Rosenthal's path to happiness are the same! *Success and happiness will come when we actively treasure and care about the people in our lives. And the more people we bring into our hearts, the more successful and happy we will be.* That is the underlying message from everyone in this chapter. It is our relationships with the people closest to us that matter most. So let's consider what we can do to improve our relationships with our partners, adult children, grandchildren, and friends.

RELATIONSHIPS WITH PARTNERS

The interviews with people in the Retirement Puzzle Cohort reveal three actions we can take to revitalize our relationships with our partners during retirement: respect individuality, open up, and revive our feelings.

Respect Individuality. One of the perplexing questions I had when I started to research retirement living was, "How can couples live together compatibly 24/7?" The answer came from Mary Elliott and Neil Rosenthal: Most can't.

As Rosenthal observed, we each need our own sense of self. To feel complete we must have our own identities, goals, interests, activities, friendships, and involvements. Before retirement, we were accustomed to a certain amount of independence. The desire for that independence will not mysteriously disappear just because we — or our partners — stop working full-time.

People are different, and we each have our own unique needs. When problems arise, men typically withdraw and women think out loud. While men want to be left alone, women want to be heard. Men avoid vulnerability where women seek understanding and support. In recent years, much has been written about these differences. But the essential point is that each of us has needs that must be respected. To have a sense of self, we must be able to *be* ourselves. And we need time, space, and privacy to do that. When we don't have that — when we are together with our partners too much of the time — their exhaustive presence can descend like a cloud. The relationship will likely become burdensome for one or both partners.

To revitalize the relationship, we must begin by respecting each other's individuality. We must develop our own interests and support the rights of our partners to develop and enjoy theirs. The time we spend apart in our chosen endeavors will stimulate us, while our partners find their own sense of fulfillment. When we rejoin after these experiences, both people will be refreshed and reenergized. Each will bring vitality back to the relationship.

Vibrant relationships are able to survive the natural conflict between individuality and companionship because there is a mutual respect for privacy and independence. As Ernest Hemingway's mother, Grace, told her family, "I love you all, but I have to have a rest from you now and then if I am to go on loving. If I could wish for one great gift for each of my children, I think it would be that they each might find a mate who understands this need."

In respecting individuality, it is also essential that we avoid trying to manipulate, control, or change our partners. Healthy relationships are based on the conviction that each person is equally important, that differences should be encouraged, and that each should have their needs met. If these values are missing, both partners suffer because the relationship has not been allowed to develop to its potential.

One of the great joys of retirement is that we have time to enjoy being with our partners, unencumbered by the daily pressures that previously intruded into our lives. To benefit from this opportunity, however, we must realize that our relationship will be richer, fuller, and more rewarding if we don't over-impose on one another.

Open Up. While it is appropriate to expand our horizons by spending time apart in personal activities, it is also important that when we are together we *be* together. As we enter retirement, most of us in long-term relationships share the benefits of mature love. While young love is characterized by excitement, freshness, and energy, mature love is blessed with richness. With mature love come wholeness, comfort, and confidence.

Despite that, Neil Rosenthal is right — many of us have not allowed our relationships to develop as fully as possible. We hold certain feelings in. We fail to open up to one another because we are afraid of offending or hurting our partners. We don't want to make waves or cause anger. And we don't want to expose our vulnerabilities and insecurities. We reason that life will be smoother if we leave sensitive issues untouched, simmering below the surface. In doing so, we may prevent some feelings from surfacing, but we will also prevent our relationship from becoming as honest and trusting as it can be. And we will unintentionally create a pattern of stilted communication that will remain a barrier between us until we decide to tear it down. If Neil Rosenthal is right — if honest, intimate, sincere relationships are a key to our happiness — why do we often prevent that from happening with the people who are closest to us? It really doesn't make any sense.

If we want better relationships with our partners, we have to open up, and we have to create an environment in which our partners are invited to do so as well. One suggestion is to take the lead by disclosing thoughts about yourself or your past that you have held inside. This will be non-threatening for your partner and will help define new boundaries for your relationship. Encourage your partner to do the same. By doing so, you will create an atmosphere of deeper trust and confidence. You will be able to build on this foundation by talking about other issues you have previously avoided.

As openness increases, subjects that have been hidden from sight will surface. And the more open our communication becomes, the more complete our relationships will be. To be emotionally close, we must tell the truth, and we must be empathic, non-defensive listeners. The benefits are miraculous. We learn to avoid hidden agendas and live in the present. We regularly show that we value our partners. We learn to discuss and resolve issues that affect our lives together. We become more actively involved in joint decision-making. We prevent little things from festering. Our patience improves. We become more understanding and supportive. We find greater joy in our partner's successes and become more sensitive to his or her concerns. We face issues that have been ignored or taken for granted. We get on the same page!

People in the Retirement Puzzle Cohort have identified five questions that assess the quality of a couple's relationship. They are:

- Do they talk about important things?

- Are they honest with each other?

- Do they share?

- Have they resolved differences?

- Are their values compatible?

Consider how being more open with each other affects the answers to these questions. By opening up and encouraging our partners to do so as well, we revitalize our relationships. We take them to another level that will tremendously improve our retirement experience.

Revive Our Feelings. Mature love has wondrous advantages over young love, but some things are often sacrificed during the transition. What happened to fun and spontaneity? Where did romance go? Excitement, freshness, and energy may have been hallmarks of young love, but must they be banished simply because we are older?

Early in our marriage, I frequently gave Gayla flowers, and she hid little notes in my suitcase when I went away on business trips. What happened? Did the novelty wear off? Probably. But I suspect that the real reason things changed is that we became kid-centered, and our personal relationship slipped into the background. Our kids became the focus of our attention. We talked about them, worried about them, and did whatever we could think of to be good parents. As Jo Kearney explained, kids and grandkids often occupy the center stage in our lives.

But just because our children have become important to us does not mean that we have to let go of the joys of being a couple. Happiness in retirement comes when we take our relationships off automatic pilot. We need to relearn how to treat our partners as though they're special—because they are. Otherwise, why would we still be together?

Each of us is in charge of our own emotions. We cannot *make* anyone else happy; we can only help set the stage for them. We should not take ourselves too seriously, but we should take our relationship with our partners seriously—because a vibrant partnership will lead to happiness. The key is to genuinely care about our partner's feelings and regularly show our sincerity. We should take time to look at our relationship through our partner's eyes to find ways to build a deeper friendship. When we ask how they are doing, when we do something special, and when we bring laughter, excitement and cheerfulness into the home, the relationship comes alive and both partners enjoy life more fully.

RELATIONSHIPS WITH ADULT CHILDREN

Nobody ever told us when our role as parents would change, but it did — or should have. When our kids were little, our role was to *care for them*. By the time they became adults, our role was to *care about them*. This distinction is important.

Since very small children need to be protected, cared for, and told what to do, we learned to take charge. We made their decisions, solved their problems, and rescued them when they were threatened. We became proficient at managing their lives, just as we managed our own. And it made us feel good to be loving, responsible parents.

When kids grow up, however, this parenting style becomes inappropriate. Kids need to learn how to take care of themselves, and parents need to let go. As Jo Kearney pointed out, this is particularly difficult when we see our kids making decisions that we believe are wrong. But if we want to have healthy relationships with our adult children, we have to allow them to live as they see fit. When we interfere and manipulate, we build barriers and create distrust. But when we recognize that we are no longer in control — when we respect them as adults, show unconditional love and support, listen to them, and provide advice only when asked — we can become trusted, reliable friends. If we have done these things, we will have helped build the base for a wonderful, ongoing adult relationship.

All of this is fine in theory and usually works in practice. Unfortunately, theory and reality are sometimes at odds. Some kids never leave the nest. Others experience difficulties — like divorces — in the real world and return. Some are unsuccessful at managing their own affairs. Others run into financial problems and cry out for assistance. In short, the separation that was expected to happen when the kids became adults never fully materialized. They remain more reliant upon us — emotionally and financially — than was expected. This creates stress for everyone involved. How do we deal with it?

There is no definitive answer. The personalities, circumstances, and dynamics differ far too greatly from one situation to the next. But I learned an important lesson from Mike Sargent, one of the financial advisors we met in Chapter Three. Mike observed that people often make the mistake of only considering their current emotions and sense of responsibility when confronted with difficult family decisions. They don't look beyond. As parents, they try to solve their kids' problems rather than provide a loving environment in which the kids can take responsibility for themselves.

We should not allow the difficulties facing any of our adult children to become disastrous for other family members. Taking care of ourselves needs to be a priority, because the last thing we want is to become an emotional or financial burden on our other children. Thus, it is important for us to weigh all factors when we determine how difficult family situations should be handled.

As has often been said, "once a parent always a parent." To love our kids is as ingrained as anything in our being. When they have joined us in adulthood, we need to express that love appropriately, and they need to take responsibility for living their own lives.

RELATIONSHIPS WITH GRANDCHILDREN

Think of grandchildren as little teachers. More than anybody, they have the ability to put our lives in perspective. They are the hope of the future and the unabated love of the present. The purity of their joy, sadness, energy, fatigue, enthusiasm, and curiosity reminds us that our lives have been worth living — if for no other reason than to help make sure that they got here.

Grandchildren give us one last opportunity to play a role in the unfolding future. Their parents have the job of raising them. We only have the job of loving them. It is not a bad task. In fact, most of us find that it rivals all other joys that we experience at this stage of our lives.

There is one note of caution, however. Just as our kids raced through life and were soon making their own way, so too will these little ones. There is only a short window of opportunity to develop the relationship with them that will last through the remainder of our lives. We should not let it pass.

RELATIONSHIPS WITH FRIENDS

In retirement, friendships are more important than ever. The daily interaction we had with people at work is behind us. Time is plentiful and our days are unstructured. Friends allow us to escape loneliness and isolation. They help us maintain our sense of self and adapt to the changes we face. They contribute to our physical and psychological well-being and add to our life satisfaction. So it is easy to understand why the ability to maintain old and build new friendships is one of the key predictors of success in retirement.

While friendships are important for everyone, they are particularly important for people who are single. And half the people who are married when they enter retirement will survive their spouses and end up single. Since most older people do not live with their children, friends have a greater influence on their morale than do family members.

How do you revitalize friendships? Simply by doing what friends do. Like Jo Kearney said, friends provide a carefree, joyous connection without expectations. Men and women may do that in different ways, but the common denominators are camaraderie, sharing, support, and trust. To be a friend is to be accepting and non-judgmental. Friends provide meaningful discussion and stimulation. Friends show their interest in one another and are supportive in times of adversity. Friends do voluntarily what family members feel obligated to do.

CONCLUDING THOUGHTS

In Chapter One, we found that by becoming adaptable, positive, and involved, we develop an attitudinal foundation for achieving happiness and fulfillment. As it turns out, those are the same qualities we need to revitalize our relationships. We have to adapt to changing circumstances, maintain a positive outlook, and stay involved with the people who are closest to us.

Partners, children, grandchildren, and friends are only some of the people in our lives, and the way we approach those relationships should be applied to others as well. All close relationships are built on caring and trust. When we genuinely care about the people we know and show our sincerity, we receive so much more in return. Maintaining quality relationships truly is a key to lasting happiness.

SEVEN

THE FIFTH CHALLENGE:
Maintaining Self-Esteem

(It all starts inside.)

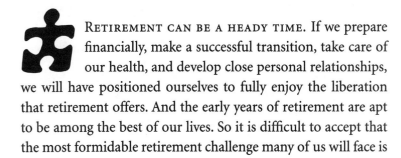

RETIREMENT CAN BE A HEADY TIME. If we prepare financially, make a successful transition, take care of our health, and develop close personal relationships, we will have positioned ourselves to fully enjoy the liberation that retirement offers. And the early years of retirement are apt to be among the best of our lives. So it is difficult to accept that the most formidable retirement challenge many of us will face is looming ever closer.

With retirement comes aging. And aging brings diminishments. If we don't respond properly, these diminishments can put our self-esteem at risk. Self-esteem is an inner feeling of competence, relevance, and pride. When we have self-esteem, we feel good about who we are. We have confidence in our ability to change our lives. And we can be adaptable, positive, and involved. Maintaining our self-esteem is crucial because we cannot achieve lasting happiness and fulfillment without it.

Self-esteem is formed early in life and is fine-tuned over the years. As the overly optimistic fantasies of our youth evolve into more realistic life goals, our self-esteem and expectations adapt accordingly. For most of us, by the time we reach retirement age our self-esteem has been battle-tested and has made its peace with reality. We have become comfortable within ourselves.

But as we move through retirement—particularly the elder years—our self-esteem can be assailed by ever-increasing losses and fears. Threats may arise from reduced feelings of accomplishment, loss of purpose, loss of stamina and strength, failing health, slower reaction times, declining mental acuity, the death of loved ones, fear of pain, and fear of the unknown. The results can be disastrous. If we lose our self-esteem, we will probably become spectators rather than players.

Maintaining self-esteem is the fifth and most vital challenge we face. Those who struggle with this challenge are likely to become grouchy and depressed—and few people will want to be around them. Yet those who overcome it often become an inspiration to the people who know them. Maintaining self-esteem is worth the effort.

The first five people we meet in this chapter provide different views on maintaining self-esteem during retirement. Then we hear from a nationally renowned authority on retirement and aging who helps us put everything in perspective.

We start with Ty Kaus and Jean Barr. Pay particular attention to the way they continue to challenge themselves in retirement and how their passionate approach to living reinforces their strong sense of self-esteem.

Ty Kaus – *Conquering Adversity*

TY KAUS LEARNED HOW TO confront self-esteem issues and overcome adversity early in life. Ty contracted polio when he was five and has been relegated to braces and crutches or a wheelchair for the past seventy years. He was physically unable to attend school from the first through the eighth grades, but he was not deterred. He ended up attending Duke University, where he was editor of the campus magazine, played principal oboe in the symphony, and graduated Phi Beta Kappa. In 1953, he married an incredibly supportive wife, giving him the opportunity to pursue his wide-ranging interests. In New York City, he became a copywriter, creative director, columnist, magazine editor, and a founder of the Copywriters' Club of New York. At twenty-eight, he became a Life Master in tournament-bridge. Later, he took up wheelchair sports, going on to win more than 300 trophies and medals in racing, swimming, bowling, table tennis, javelin, discus, shot put, and tennis. He set the world record in breaststroke for Paralympians, was National Wheelchair Table Tennis Champion for thirteen years, was a member of five U.S. Paralympic and Pan American sports teams, and was inducted into the National Wheelchair Sports Hall of Fame in 1988.

Ty's competitive nature surfaced early in life. "I had parents who did not coddle me, who encouraged me and let me be myself as much as I could be. I developed a sense of independence that many badly handicapped people don't have, maybe because they rely on too many caregivers. I enjoy challenges, and I've always wanted to prove to myself that I could do things well. I guess I'm just very competitive.

"When I was five years old, just before I had polio, I set school records for my age group in the hundred-yard dash and high jump. When I got polio, my aspirations for sports went out the window until I found out in my late thirties that people were participating in wheelchair sports. I saw in the paper that guys in wheelchairs were bowling, and I immediately knew that I wanted to do that. I took a few lessons and then I started to compete. The second year, I finished second in the Nationals. But that was just the start! When I talked to some of the other bowlers, I found out about the other great things that they were doing. They were playing table tennis and all other kinds of sports. So I got heavily involved in most of them. Back then, you could compete in the Nationals in many different events. I did, and I won trophies and medals in a lot of them. But gradually, as wheelchair sports became more intense and more competitive, it became important to specialize. I couldn't be a generalist anymore. So I specialized in swimming and table tennis."

Ty's success led to another activity that was particularly fulfilling. "I went around to hospitals and rehabilitation centers giving motivational speeches and demonstrations of wheelchair sports to newly injured kids, trying to inspire them and show them that life is not over just because they're in a wheelchair. They have their lives ahead of them. They have to focus on the things they can do, not on what they can't do. They have to make the best of it."

The competitive drive did not stop when Ty retired. "I worked for forty-four years in advertising and publishing. It was a high-pressure career—every single day of the year including weekends and holidays. I was constantly worrying about the next deadline. Then, when I retired, the pressure was gone. But the drive was still there. I couldn't cut it off; it was still in my nature. So I had to spread it out into other things. I couldn't all of a sudden say, 'Hey, I don't have to worry about anything anymore; I am just going to do nothing.' That's not the way I function, and I don't think many other people do. You either maintain the type of high-pressure life that you had or you get so frustrated that you start going downhill. You may not be operating at the same level or doing the same things, but you have to keep your interests up and stay involved."

Ty has done that. "The thing is, I have the God-given gift of being interested in almost everything. When I retired, I thought I wanted to get a Ph.D. in nutrition because I already had a strong background in that area. But when I realized how time-consuming that would be, I decided that I didn't want to do anything that would so completely absorb me that I couldn't do anything else. I'm just too interested in what's going on in the world. I would get very bored doing just one thing."

Ty's wide range of activities reflects this attitude. He has coached and played tennis, played and beat most able-bodied people who have opposed him in table tennis, authored three books, served on fourteen residential committees, composed and performed music, been an activist for his local disability task force, served as a wheelchair consultant, written and edited articles and newsletters, created and funded a video library, lectured and performed before various groups, mentored children, and been active in his church and Rotary.

"What frustrates me tremendously is that I don't have enough time to read what I want to. One of my majors in college was English literature, and I wish I had the time to read good books. But I don't. I do make time for my writing. It is one of the things that really keeps me going. I've written three books, two of original haiku poetry and one of original 'punecdotes.' I've got many more books in my head that I am working on, including twelve children's books. I'm a wordsmith; I just love the written word, and as I get older I am going to write more. Sure, I miss competitive sports, but I have sublimated it to my writing now. Writing books has just started for me. Now I am consumed by it."

Ty is also concerned about making the world more manageable for people with disabilities. "I've been involved with the Disability Task Force for nine years. It took three and a half years to get one of the restaurants here wheelchair-accessible. With a lot of help from other task force members, I finally got them to put a ramp in and a wheelchair bathroom on the first floor. I've been involved in making other business establishments more accessible and have been working for two years to make sure that the parks and recreation areas accommodate physically handicapped people."

Ty is financially secure, but he has found that at this stage of his life material things are of little importance. Instead, making sure that his daughter and her family are properly prepared for the future is a high priority. "I'm not rich, but I have more than enough for our lifestyle. We have modest tastes. We don't buy expensive clothes. We don't go out to dinner very often. I'm driving a thirteen-year-old car, which is just perfect. I'll probably never get rid of it. Because of our physical problems, we don't travel anymore. So, what are we going to spend money for? We spend it to help the kids. We put money in their college funds. There is a lot of satisfaction in that."

Jean Barr – *Put Your Buttons in a Row*

WHEN MOST PEOPLE would have been looking forward to retirement, Jean Barr started a business. Money was one of her early motivations. But now the company provides relationships and relevancy that enrich her life.

While her kids were growing up, Jean was a housewife, volunteer, and member of Junior League. Her husband, Jim, was a CPA. It appeared that her life would continue to unfold along traditional lines. She wanted more than that. She still does.

In the early 1970s when her kids went to college, she did a favor for someone that led to a life-changing opportunity. "One of my brother's novelty company customers needed buttons for ski sweaters that her customers were knitting. When she heard that I was going to Italy for my husband's reunion with the Tenth Mountain Army Division, she asked me to find some unique buttons. We also ended up going to Vienna, and I bought every silver button in one of the department stores there. I sold them all as soon as I returned. After that I decided I was going to get into the button business."

In the early years, the buttons were packaged on the Barr's basement ping-pong table. That changed. Now her company, JHB International, is one of the country's leading button importers and exporters. "We grew by importing from various places around the world and picking up retail accounts. Then we decided to design a line of JHB copyrighted designs. At first, I was the only designer, but now my son does some of the designs. What we are known for in the world market is novelty buttons. We import from over one hundred factories around the world and export to about forty countries."

Jean's son, Jay, has become JHB's president. But Jean, now in her eighties, remains the CEO and goes to work five or six days a week. She wouldn't have it any other way. "My husband says that sometimes I drive him crazy because I think about buttons all the time. He says I even think about how to turn sunsets into button designs. I guess I've gotten to the point where I see buttons in everything. But that is part of what makes it fun for me.

"Jay and I try to take at least one international trip per year to the Far East and one to Europe. When we go to the Far East, we usually go to China, Hong Kong, and Taipei together. He does the Philippines by himself, while I go to Japan. Then sometimes my husband and I will mix in some business and vacation trips. A few years ago, we went to the Galapagos Islands, and I developed a new line of sea animal buttons.

"Basically, I'm a gypsy. I love to travel, and I never get over the pleasure of it. Sometimes the flights—particularly to the Far East—get pretty long. But one of the reasons our international business is growing so well is that we have a long track record with factories all over the world, and we have the most extensive product line available. We are now reaping the benefits of relationships developed over a lot of years.

"I am very fortunate. I am healthy and still involved and still thinking all the time about how to make the business better. I think that makes a big difference with older people. The ones who are stimulated and excited about what they are doing are so much better off than those who just sit around and become

bored. I know that the job helps keep me young, at least relatively speaking. And I think that staying involved helps keep me
mentally alert.

"Some people may think I'm a workaholic. But really I am
just dedicated to what I am doing. I love to get up in the morning. I start every day by swimming, and then I go to work. I just
love all of it—the challenges, the people, and the excitement. I
love to see the business grow. I love knowing that we have created jobs for so many people—all around the world. I love
knowing that our customers get such satisfaction from our
products. So I tell people, 'I am never going to retire the way
other people do, but someday I may sell buttons to angels.'"

One of the many reasons Jean finds the business so fascinat-
ing is that she has become multilingual. "JHB has given me the
opportunity to meet people and learn languages I never would
have. I speak German and Spanish, some Italian and Japanese,
and a little bit of French. Certainly, this has made the business
that much more fun.

"It's a very exciting and significant thing to think that we have
been able to make a mark in the international market and to see
that it is still growing. To me, that is a great thrill. But even more,
to have the opportunity to become acquainted with people from
so many different countries and cultures has been very rewarding. My life has been so full because of it. Every morning when
I come into the office I have faxes and emails from around the
world that keep me connected. And in so many cases, we have
developed close relationships. In fact, one man from Paris calls
me his American grandmother. It's just wonderful. We have lots
of those special relationships. It goes on and on and on. It's just
like having an extended family. I love it!

"I have grandchildren who I really love being with. And we
have a home on the Maine coast. During the summer I com-
mute back and forth every eight or ten days, and when I am in
Maine, I enjoy spending time out on our cruiser. I used to be a

gourmet cook, but I don't cook at home as often as I did. I still love cooking out on that cruiser, though.

"I keep up with some of the organizations that I used to be involved with, but I am no longer very active. Don't you think that is really common among people who have been entrepreneurs? That they are just really dedicated to their businesses, their employees, and their customers? That they have a passion for their businesses that isn't duplicated in other parts of their lives? My brother is still going strong and is just as dedicated to his business as I am to mine. At this point, I don't think either of us is going to change!"

Ty and Jean have a passion for living and a desire to challenge themselves that defines who they are. John Beynon, Rosalie Beehler, and Kayrene Pearson have also thrived on challenges. But in recent years they have personally experienced some the effects of aging, and there have been serious health problems in their families. Note the role that their values, beliefs, and love have played in sustaining them through their difficulties.

John Beynon –
When Expectations and Reality Diverge

AFTER GRADUATING WITH A DEGREE in architecture from MIT, John Beynon worked on a couple of education projects funded by the Ford Foundation. In 1964, he was working as a research assistant at Stanford University when he was offered an opportunity to go to Paris for two years to head a research project on alternative school designs for the United Nations Educational, Scientific, and Cultural Organization (UNESCO). The temporary assignment stretched into a challenging overseas career with responsibilities all around the globe.

Initially, John was responsible for developing alternative approaches to designing school buildings in Third World countries. Ultimately, he became the director for all of the technical

assistance that UNESCO provided in the field of education—
including educational planning, school building, curriculum
development, and teacher training. For most of his career he was
based in Paris, where he and his wife, Valerie, raised their kids.
When John retired, he did not have a clear vision of what would
come next.

"Valerie was convinced I was a workaholic because I worked
every night until 9:00 or 10:00. She was afraid that I was going
to crash and burn. When the time came for retirement, I hadn't
planned for it. I had been too involved in my work. And with
retirement came the usual questions about what to do. Paris was
too expensive, and our four children lived in the States. So we
came back to America.

"It took us a while to get settled, and at first this was an
extremely lonesome place. We had been overseas for thirty-two
years, and we didn't have friends here. I think what saved me is
that I got involved with the local chapter of the United Nations
Association (UNA)—a grassroots organization that supports
what the United Nations does. The people involved with UNA
are knowledgeable and interested in international affairs. Since
they had interests similar to mine, finding them after my first
couple of years back here was a major breakthrough for me.
Being able to interact with them helps me keep a perspective on
the world and on domestic politics."

John gets more than camaraderie and mental stimulation
from his UNA chapter; he gets the satisfaction of knowing that
he is still a contributing member of society. "One of the things
we did was get involved in the United Nations' Adopt-a-
Minefield program. It raises funds to support the U.N.'s effort to
increase awareness about and remove landmines around the
globe. We created a coalition of groups that was able to raise
$100,000 for this program. We also organized book and
fundraising drives for schools in Afghanistan. So far, we have
been able to send 2,500 university-level textbooks and $68,000

to nine different schools. Getting involved like that feels good. Really good!

"Then I got a call from UNESCO. They said that they were sending a mission to Afghanistan for two weeks to work on the higher education system and asked if I would be interested in going along to look after the buildings component. I flew to Paris, got the briefing, and went on to Kabul as part of the thirteen-person mission. That resulted in a published book that identified $100 million in university-level projects. Now they are meeting with potential donors.

"After the Afghanistan project, UNESCO called again and said they wanted me to train education administrators in Cambodia. So now I am putting that project together. There is a real feeling of satisfaction that comes from knowing you are making a contribution."

John's interest in international education started when he was growing up in Nevada. "I suppose these are values that my mother drummed into my head when I was very young, but I am very anti-racist and anti-intolerant in general. Because I was small and not cowboy-tough, I experienced some intolerance when I was growing up. And I didn't like it at all. I have a tremendous empathy for the black community, and I think that translated quite easily into working in the Third World. I learned early that not everything that happens in America is perfect. My conclusion was that everybody has something to teach and everybody has something to learn. I have always had an attitude that we should do more to take advantage of that.

"I can't stand not to learn. Now that I am retired, one of the things I do is read newspapers for about two hours every day. I never had time for that before, and I have learned a tremendous amount about American policymaking and American politics. The UNA chapter has a discussion group run by a retired social engineer who lives up the street, and we talk about globalization and disarmament and other subjects that we are all interested in.

I have also learned a lot about information technology that I never knew before. I have found all of that very interesting, and it has kept me learning."

As stimulating as retirement has been, John has faced risks as well. "The biggest risks are hidden in the unexpected: health issues. My health is fine, but Valerie's is not. And that is something we didn't see coming and definitely were not prepared for. To the degree that we did any retirement planning, it was done based on how we felt at the time. We had fanciful ideas that were not well thought-out. We couldn't imagine how different we might feel when we got older. People do go through different phases in retirement, but couples don't necessarily go through those phases in lockstep. That means that both have to be flexible and patient. And not everybody is—particularly those of us who are driven to be active. So that is a challenge we've had to face.

"Early in our married life, we learned how important it was to not treat marriage as an institution where each member goes halfway when dealing with issues. Successful marriages are a 70-70 proposition where both partners love the other enough to go the extra mile. This is never more evident than when health problems enter the picture.

"Obviously, there are also some financial risks, but they are not the major issue once you accept a more modest standard of living. The more problematic issue is becoming old and grumpy and losing your spirit of happiness. And that is what will happen if you're not careful."

In John's mind, the path we must take to prevent that is clear. "You stand tall and don't let a negative attitude get in your way. There have been moments—due to Valerie's health problems— that we have been under a lot of stress. It takes patience, and sometimes you have to go back and rethink things. You have to rewrite the scenarios. With life comes change. When the last kid goes off to college, you sit across the table from each other wondering 'What do we talk about now?' And you have to figure out how to adjust. When health issues change your life, you have to do the same thing. There is no other acceptable choice.

"Along with the health thing, which you can't plan for but should keep in mind, there is the danger that you will get to the point where you don't know how to contribute. So far, that has not been a problem for me because I know what I can do, and I am doing it. But I am not quite sure I will deal with the next chapter of my life so well. That concerns me because if you're not contributing, you're only observing. And if you are only observing, how are you going to feel good about yourself? At some age, that may be okay. But I suspect there is a big risk of becoming depressed."

John can see some signs of change. "There have been little hints. I am sixty-eight, and I'm at a point where mental acuity begins to decline. I have experienced some short-term memory losses, like forgetting where I put certain files. I know that the work I am doing is good, but I am not quite as quick as I was. So I feel more challenged, and sometimes I am not quite as satisfied with my work as I used to be. But I think it is really important to keep finding new objectives that are achievable. You can't live in the past because you will not be able to do all of the things you used to do. So you better change the target. But whatever you do, you have to stay involved and keep challenging yourself to learn and grow."

Like the others in the Retirement Puzzle Cohort who are positive and motivated, John is a good role model for all of us. But he is not eager to claim that title. "I suppose I would find it a little bit pretentious, but that doesn't necessarily mean I don't think it. For sure, I have what I refer to as Beynon's Theory of Eternal Optimism. The world continues to get better. Even the poorest, most miserable countries are trying to get better. And many are succeeding. If you concentrate on getting better, eventually something positive will happen. With that philosophy, I have always tried to focus on what can I do to make things better. I don't think that will ever change."

Rosalie Beehler – *Surviving the Unthinkable*

ROSALIE BEEHLER IS IN HER MID-EIGHTIES and lives in an assisted-living center. Until now, she has never shared parts of her life story. It is easy to understand why.

Rosalie was brought up as a Presbyterian in McPherson, Kansas, a county that she recalls was about half Swedish and half Mennonite. Rosalie's father was a dentist and gentleman farmer. He accumulated seven farms in Texas on which oil was discovered. Rosalie's family was financially sound through the Depression, when most other families in the community were struggling. At McPherson College, she met and fell in love with Orville Beehler, who came from a totally different background.

After Orville's father lost his Idaho farm in the 1930s, he worked in the apple orchards and at the apple packing plant. The family belonged to the Church of the Brethren, one of the three historic peace churches—along with Quakers and Mennonites. After college, Orville and Rosalie became teachers. But with the low pay, they did not have enough money to marry. When the U.S. got involved in World War II and Orville received his draft papers, they faced an even greater challenge.

For Rosalie, the memories are still vivid. "Orville was a conscientious objector during World War II and was in public service throughout the war. He was in five different camps with the Civilian Public Service, wherever the government decided to send him. We were married while he was being sent from one of those camps to another. The first thing we did together on our honeymoon was go to work in a mental hospital. Being responsible for thirty patients who were mentally and physically ill was a challenge for me. I really grew up.

"But conscientious objectors were looked down on in those

days. In some ways, I think that was the experience that made me who I am. The first day I went into the dining room, everybody got up and left. The employees weren't going to sit with conscientious objectors. One time, a patient even threw a whole tray of fruit at me. We never knew what each day would bring, but it just made me stronger.

"Things were difficult during the war. But I had two babies before the war was over and three more after the war, four boys and a girl. I never did go back to teaching, other than some substituting. Orville was hired as a teacher after the war, and for the first five years everything went really well. But then he came down with acute hepatitis, and when he went back to work he was still a nervous wreck. From then on he had some mental problems. I think it became noticeable after the hepatitis, but it probably started with the treatment he received during the war. It was really demeaning to be an outcast in society for six years. He lost faith in himself and in other human beings. He became increasingly depressed. As a result, he didn't treat our kids as well as he should have. There was abuse involved, but I didn't want other people to know about it.

"I was scared, but I still loved him. It was frustrating. I wanted him to get some professional help, but he resisted. I thought a counselor for the whole family was what we needed because one person's illness affects the whole family. Finally, the child welfare department decided that my daughter should not live in the same house with my husband. I was devastated. I spent many nights out on the back steps crying because I didn't want any of the family to know how devastated I was. I had to threaten Orville with divorce before he agreed to get some help. But even that was difficult. After about ten tries, we finally found a wonderful psychiatrist.

"Orville was a good teacher, really talented. In fact, many people said that he was the best teacher they ever had. He led church camps and was involved in all kinds of crafts. He was in the choir at the Presbyterian church for thirty-five years. But his mental problems got worse after he retired. In a way, retirement was his undoing. All he wanted to do was sit in his chair. I spent a lot of time taking care of him, but there really wasn't anything I could do to change the situation. After a while he was diagnosed with dementia. Later on he started falling down. That was the beginning of the end. He had to move into a health care unit, and then he died about a year and a half ago."

Rosalie's faith helped her survive the difficult times. "When you get married, you can't have any idea of what you will go through. You don't know a person until you have lived with them, and we all change over time. I'm no angel, but I wanted the best for my kids. And I think the way I was brought up was important. My religion helped save me. I think a strong faith in something larger than yourself is very important. It also helped to remember back to when we were younger, when he was handsome and capable. I tried to forget about the frustrations and live with the wonderful memories.

"Fortunately, the kids turned out really well. As they grew older, they understood what the problems were. And they are a wonderful bunch. They have always been there to help me. They either see me or call me all the time. Even during the last months of Orville's life, the son who had endured the most abuse was good to him. He went to Orville and told him that it was all right to die, that it was part of life. And it was good that he could be going home."

For Rosalie, becoming a caregiver to such a changed man was difficult. "You have to have a lot of love. I'll tell you that. It's difficult. I was fortunate that I was strong enough not to fall into depression. I know a lot of people in similar situations who have become angry and depressed. But an interesting thing happened during the last few years. I met several other women whose husbands had mental problems. We became very close friends because we understood what one another were going through.

We could talk to each other about our problems when we could not talk to anyone else.

"If you end up taking care of your husband because his health declines, remember that it takes a lot of love and a lot of forgiving. That's not easy, and you will always wonder about when it's going to be over. When it finally did happen, I felt it was time for him to have a rest from the torments of this world.

"You know, I've never talked about a lot of this before. I guess I just figured that was life, and I don't want people to feel sorry for me. But there's an old Japanese saying that says, 'If a woman be loved, hated, and envied, her life is worth living.' I've always told people that I thought I qualified."

Kayrene Pearson – *The More You Give*

KAYRENE PEARSON WAS RAISED in Condon, Oregon, and graduated from Oregon State University in 1955. "I grew up with a liberal education and a strong feeling that life was good—and also with a belief that I had an opportunity to do anything that I wanted to do." After teaching for three years, Kayrene found herself searching for answers to some of life's most challenging questions. "What is life about? Do I believe in God? Where does religion fit into my life? What do I want to do with the rest of my life?" The inquiry led her to the Pacific School of Religion in Berkeley, California, and a Master's of Divinity degree. After being ordained, she became a practicing minister and has maintained a strong interest in adult education—including biblical studies, marriage counseling, values clarification, parent effectiveness training, life transitions, and problem solving.

Kayrene and her husband, Ivar, raised two children. Since retiring in 1995, she has remained active. "I figured that I could carry on my ministry anywhere and didn't need to be paid a salary. So I have done some preaching, and I put together adult education programs for several different churches—First

Congregational Church, UCC; First Methodist Church; and Community United Church of Christ. I also served as the pastoral care minister for the Unitarian Universalist Fellowship while their minister was on sabbatical.

"Early in retirement you have more energy than you do later on, and you need to take advantage of that. Exercise is a very important part of keeping energized. And I think being social, keeping your relationships, and staying involved are also really important. I took courses in meditation and world religions to keep my mind active and challenged. I learned that you can train your mind to be more disciplined, and I expanded my understanding of religion. I have never felt that Christianity was the only way to God, and I enjoy having the opportunity to share that with other people. You know, sometimes we become very narrow as we age. It is really important to keep opening ourselves to new ideas."

However, not everybody is so flexible. "I think personality is a big factor. People who have shown that they can make changes in their lives before they retire are usually more successful at making the transition to becoming elderly. But that is not a guarantee. Everyone is unique. I think having faith that God is a spirit within you—that nurtures you in times of trial and loneliness and loss—is very helpful. Growing older is a difficult adjustment for most people. You don't just get over it in one year.

"Attitude about life is so critical. When I needed to be around because my husband spent nine months on the couch after surgery, some of my friends said to me, 'Isn't that just awful? You are literally a prisoner in your apartment.' But I said, 'You know, it isn't! There are always good things that come about.' Our relationship developed to a new level. He gained some respect for me because I was taking care of him when he had always thought of himself as the caretaker. And it helped me because it was a new challenge. I felt that if I could meet that challenge, I could meet the next one too. We have a stronger relationship now.

"Some of my friends have said to me, 'I have been so worried about what is going to happen to my husband and me when we have to face that.' I told them, 'You have the opportunity to learn new ways of coping rather than becoming resentful and bitter. It's up to you.'

"There is a big difference when you are not healthy—when you are limited. When your health changes you have to have an open mind. As your energy slows down, your social activity slows down, and you can't make the contributions that you used to. That is a huge adjustment. I've always felt that giving back is very important in life. And I continue to feel that it does more for me than it does for anybody else. When I teach a class at the YWCA, I learn more than the class participants do. I truly believe that the more you give, the more you receive. But the hard part is that when you become old and can no longer do this you may feel diminished. You want to continue giving, but you can't do it in the same way. That is very hard. I am moving into that stage. I can't call on people like I used to, and I can't teach like I used to. And those have been an integral part of my self-image. So I have to adjust.

"I have always said that life is about setting limits. And as you grow older, there will be more and more limits that you don't have control over. If you are aware of this, you become more creative about what you can do within these limits. But no matter how old you are you have to take the initiative to bring other people into your life and make things happen.

"One lady I call on is ninety-seven and in a wheelchair. She is a wonderful role model. She isn't happy about being so old and having so many limitations, but she is alert. She reads. She listens to talking books. She treats the people who care for her well. She is able to do so much for someone her age. It's remarkable. At that age there are so many challenges, but some people manage really well. They find hope in new ways. Even if they can't get outside, they can look out the window and see the garden, hear the birds, and watch the changing of the seasons. All of those things help give life perspective. But the people who continue to fight aging often become bitter and depressed. They can end up with very few friends and social contacts."

Kayrene is beginning to experience some of the frustrations of aging, but she is also learning how to adapt. "It is very difficult. I can't do some of the things I used to do, and our daughter doesn't hesitate to remind me about it. But there are some advantages too. She is capable and a good thinker. There are certain situations that are difficult for me to face, and she steps in to help. Our son is also supportive. It is comforting knowing that they are there.

"The health losses are the biggest factor for most people. When your health begins to fail, you go through a grieving period—just like you do with a death. The body that you have known is no longer the same. It has changed. People who lose their sight have a grieving process to go through, but people who lose their hearing have an even bigger challenge. When you lose your sight, you can still communicate with people. It is harder for people who lose their hearing. They are really isolated because it is so much more difficult to communicate.

"Good health makes such a difference. And when you don't have it you are really at a loss—unless you have a very active inner life. Many of the people who pray or meditate do have an active inner life. They don't feel as lonely. Actually, they like the quiet. Other people find that writing their memoirs is helpful. That gives them something to leave behind for their families. If you don't like writing, there are other people who will listen to your life stories and write them for you.

"I believe that religion is a very important aspect of aging. I find that people who have a strong faith that God is with them—regardless of where they are—feel that somehow this spirit will continue to show them new ways of living. They may be disappointed because this is not the way that they hoped their life would end. But the spirit keeps generating. There is something very creative about this process."

Robert Atchley –
Self-Knowledge and Self-Acceptance

BOB ATCHLEY GREW UP IN OHIO, graduated from Miami University, and received his Ph.D. in sociology from American University. From 1974 to 1998 he was the director of the Scripps Gerontology Center at Miami University in Oxford, Ohio, and he is currently chair of the Department of Gerontology at Naropa University. He has authored more than a dozen books and is a former president of the American Society on Aging.

Bob's knowledge of the retirement and aging experience is exhaustive. "Retirement in our culture is a do-it-yourself project. You have a lot of freedom to decide what you want this stage of life to be about, what you want the central organizing themes to be, and how you will use your time and space. After thirty-five years of studying retirement, I can tell you people that go to the four winds in terms of what they want it to be like.

"The most ambitious study I did was one in which I started with all of the people in one town who were fifty or older on July 1, 1975. I followed that group of people for twenty years. Some were retired when the study started and others went through the retirement transition during the course of the study. I wrote a book, *Continuity and Adaptation in Aging,* based on my research. Its basic premise is that over the course of life most people learn which coping mechanisms, resources, and approaches work for them—and which don't. When life changes occur, people fall back on their proven or customary ways of coping. Who they relate to, what they think, and their physical environment all come together to serve them. While most people adapt well, there is a lot of variation from person to person.

"One of the areas of adult development that is often ignored is what happens to people when they come up against the big question about the meaning of their life. There are a lot of people who are unbelievably skilled at avoiding that question, and there are others who take advantage of the opportunity. Every time you face adversity, it is like an open enrollment period. You can either take advantage of it or wait until later.

"Many people do enroll during middle age. They go on a spiritual journey. They try to discover meaning, and they do it in an almost infinite number of ways. People find meaning in the most amazing places. If you ask a group of people to think about the spiritual experiences they have had, their responses are all over the place in terms of where they find their connection. The idea that you can only find it in church or on a mountaintop just isn't true. You can find it anywhere. And people who are advanced students of the spiritual connection do find it everywhere.

"That dimension really separates people as they go into the next phase of life. If you are really in connection with God or the Universe or the Absolute—whatever label you use for that which is a whole lot bigger than you as a human being—you have a lot of capacity to have compassion for others. And you will be better able to endure the unpleasant things that happen in life. So those spiritual resources that elders often focus on are not inconsequential.

"Aging does not invariably bring spiritual development, but it does alter the conditions of life in ways that can heighten awareness of spiritual needs. You can't make substantive generalizations. What you can say is that most people feel a need to find meaning, and they create something to fill that need. How that looks is something that each person has to discover. That's good actually. When you talk to people you find that their boats are being floated by lots of different kinds of things. That has kept me going to work for more than thirty-five years.

"I fell in love with the old ladies I studied when I was doing my dissertation because they were so clear about what was going on with them. They were the way they were, and they didn't care what anybody else thought about that. It was just wonderful dealing with people who were so relaxed and purposeful and who knew what they were here for. They had clarity about the purpose of their lives that most people my age—I was in my twenties—didn't have. There is fundamental truth in the saying, 'Know yourself, and the truth will set you free.' It took me twenty years to figure out what they had that I wanted.

"Unfortunately, in our society most people don't want to have to work through all the steps. But that is a journey that we have to go on. For some the journey is going to be long and pro-tracted and arduous. And it should be. It will never be totally over. Yet with that journey we can reach a type of consciousness from which everything is clearer."

Bob has definite ideas about what the happiest and most ful-filled retirees have in common. "They have self-knowledge and self-acceptance. They are the people who have done their home-work on themselves.

"You need to know what lights your fire or floats your boat. You have to know that so you can decide which direction you want to go—what skills you want to develop, which areas of knowledge you want to cultivate, which types of people you want to hang around with. You also need to accept yourself. But I don't think you get there by some mental exercise or by think-ing your way through it. You get there by the relentless practice of being true to who you are. It is really important to come to terms with all of the stuff you have done in your life that you wish you hadn't, because then you can move on.

"Another thing that came through loud and clear in my study was that people who lead healthy lives end up healthier.

Surprise! The people who watched their weight, watched their diet, did their exercise, and wore their seatbelts, were much less likely to be disabled in old age. If you want your body to have enough energy so that you can get excited about things, you have to take care of it. There is no way you can guarantee long-term health, but you can increase your odds.

"Also, the more you practice acting on your curiosity, the more your brain responds. The brain is constantly developing new pathways and reforming itself. If you keep stimulating it, it will keep developing.

"But you can do every preventative health thing you can think of, and if you get dementia it's still going to be bad news. And yet the people who have learned how to accept themselves—and to let go of expectations—find adapting to those changes much easier. People who don't flinch about aging and who hang around with aging people find out that there is a lot of beauty there. It is good training for learning how to relax and let things be. It brings inner peace.

"A lot of satisfaction also comes from giving something back. When your kids have moved on and you leave your employment, you have time to do that. And the idea of giving back is a good shift for most people. If you feel you have been blessed, you feel motivated to share that blessing by giving your time or your money or your nurturing. The older population does a lot of giving. It comes in different forms—childcare, financial support, encouragement, volunteering. None of these forms of giving has any moral superiority over any other. People should give whatever they can, but time and attention are especially rewarding because of the personal satisfaction that you feel."

There is also great joy to be found in providing services to non-family members. "A lot of people enjoy grandparenting more than they enjoyed parenting, because the role is much more mentor-like. You are free of the responsibilities of training and are, instead, the space-creator. That's a wonderful place to be.

Being elderly is like being a teacher. But the issue isn't so much about role modeling your personal style or your lifestyle, it is modeling your attitude—being somebody who listens, who cares about other people, and who allows other people to be themselves. To me that is the essence of parenting and mentoring.

"People have a lot of different definitions of what service is. But when they experience the joy of service—not the joy of the external acknowledgement of it, but the rewards of just doing it—they are free. The breakthrough happens when the action of service, in and of itself, becomes rewarding. That is when people feel truly joyful and appreciative and awed about where they are in their lives. They have gone beyond that materialistic place and are able to see life in a very different way."

Observations about Maintaining Self-Esteem

MANY PEOPLE FIND that the early retirement years are among the best years of their lives. Few say the same thing about very old age. The question is, how can we make aging as rich and rewarding as possible?

Aging brings diminishments. People typically experience physical deterioration, reduced mental acuity, and lower levels of energy. These degradations can lead to a loss of self-confidence, a faltering sense of purpose, and a reduced ability to contribute. We cannot stop aging or forever delay the diminishments. But we can take actions that will prevent our self-esteem from faltering.

Those of us who rebel against the inevitable are most likely to become frustrated, angry, bitter, and depressed—because the aging process will proceed whether we have our heads under our pillows or not. Resisting the unavoidable only heightens the threat to self-esteem when reality does take its toll. The least happy people tend to be inflexible and self-indulgent.

Those who age well are able to accept and adapt to reality. They see opportunities as well as limitations. They concentrate on what is possible and dismiss what is not. They focus their energies on the doable. They know that they are not powerless, just as they know that they are not in complete control. And they seek to live their lives as fully as they can.

The comments of the Retirement Puzzle interviewees reveal four strategies for bringing vitality into our lives and maintaining self-esteem, while also adapting to the unwelcome changes we must face: stretch to the limit, reach out to others, gain perspective, and become a role model.

STRETCH TO THE LIMIT

Stagnation is not the formula for a vibrant retirement life. And we shouldn't let it happen. Successful aging is the art of the possible. Throughout our retirement years, we should challenge ourselves to renew and grow. When we enrich our lives, we find value in ourselves.

Retirement living is most satisfying for those of us who make things happen, rather than waiting for things to happen — that means leading healthy lives, eating well, exercising, and keeping our minds active. It means always being on a learning curve, developing new skills and acquiring new knowledge. We should discover things that we like to do and strive to do them well. We should search for creative outlets because creativity relieves stress, stimulates health, and builds morale.

Personal growth leads to a sense of achievement, and that sense of achievement is a strong defense against waning self-esteem.

REACH OUT TO OTHERS

As we have seen, our interaction with other people is crucial to our sense of well-being. Doing things for others leads to happiness and fulfillment. It makes us feel good and whole. And when we are giving to others, we often know that they value us. So the more goodness we usher into other people's lives, the more fullness we bring into our own. That is a strong antidote for sagging self-esteem.

Caring about and giving our time to families and friends — the most important people in our lives — is particularly important. By doing so, we stay connected and avoid self-absorption. John Beynon's 70–70 proposition under which people go the extra mile for one another is a good guide and prevents us from focusing solely on ourselves.

Of course, there are other opportunities to build self-esteem by giving beyond our immediate circle of relatives and friends. Retirement presents an opportunity to acknowledge our good fortune by spending more time and energy giving something back to society. The needs and opportunities are endless. We can volunteer, mentor, form support groups, and make contributions in our communities and beyond. Providing services gives us an added reason for living.

When we give to others we will feel good about ourselves and our self-esteem will thrive.

GAIN PERSPECTIVE

Reaching out to other people helps give us perspective. But reaching out is not the whole answer. Inner freedom and personal value come from knowing who we are, what we believe, and how we fit in. As Bob Atchley said, self-knowledge and self-acceptance differentiate those who are most successful at finding happiness and fulfillment from those who aren't.

Achieving self-knowledge and self-acceptance is difficult in the absence of a well-developed belief system. Some people inherit strong religious convictions that carry them comfortably through life. But in a free society most people are exposed to alternative points of view, and that often leads to a spiritual journey in which we search for meaning and purpose. The journey may bring greater clarity. It may also be never-ending. But invariably it leads people in different directions.

Striving to understand the meaning of our lives, exploring how we fit into our world, and coming to terms with our spiritual beliefs will lead us to a sense of wholeness. And whatever our solutions are, they are an important part of preparing us for the future. Nietzsche observed, "He who has a *why* to live for can bear with almost any *how.*"

Well-developed convictions allow us to cope as we face the challenges of aging. An active inner life, including prayer or meditation, helps us put our lives in perspective and ensures that we will be better able to adjust our expectations. This is a key to successful aging, because attachment to personal expectations that are no longer feasible is a major source of unhappiness. We have to learn how to let go of unrealistic expectations and cope with unforeseen difficulties.

To age well, we must be able to accept the aging process, including both its possibilities and limitations. We must accurately appraise ourselves, reevaluate goals and expectations, and adapt appropriately. As we age, our lives will simplify in many respects. If we learn how to adapt, we will find greater peace in that simplicity.

BECOME A ROLE MODEL

Aging is not for sissies. Like it or not, we face the loss of stamina and strength, slower reaction times, and reduced mental acuity. But we do have a choice to make. We can rebel and become crotchety, or we can choose to age more gracefully. We—and all the people around us—will be better off if we choose to age gracefully by becoming good role models for the people we care about.

As good role models, we will always have purpose. We will take pride in ourselves, stay involved, and maintain positive attitudes. When faced with losses and disappointments, it is appropriate to grieve. But then we must move on. Appreciate what we do have. Count our blessings. Have compassion for those who are less fortunate. Avoid burdening others by talking endlessly about our illnesses. Reminisce to maintain perspective. Redefine our goals. Stay interested in what is going on in our world.

Self-absorption often brings isolation, while positive role modeling brings respect. There is wisdom in the saying, "If you can't change your life, change your attitude."

OLD AGE AND SELF-ESTEEM

If we stretch to the limit, reach out, gain perspective, and become good role models, we will have pride in who we are. We will be able to live with the truth, and our self-esteem will survive. But that will not minimize the challenge. As we have learned from the Retirement Puzzle Cohort, maintaining a positive attitude in the face of personal diminishments is difficult. Those who succeed are persistent, adaptable, and involved.

They stay mentally and socially engaged. When they can no longer be as physically active as they were in the past, they expand their knowledge and explore their inner worlds more thoroughly. They examine and nourish their beliefs and spirituality. When they find that they can no longer make the contributions to others that they had once made, they discover new ways to contribute. They express their love for their families and friends. They mentor by sharing their knowledge, values, and judgment.

When other people continue to play a meaningful role in our worlds, we can maintain our positive attitudes. Our dignity and self-esteem are upheld. And nothing is more important. Self-esteem is an essential step toward lasting happiness and fulfillment.

EIGHT

The Puzzle Solved

(How to get the most out of the rest of your life.)

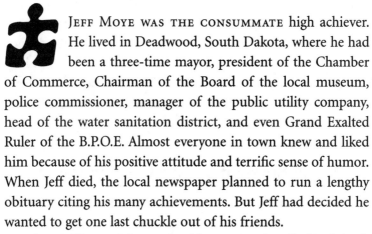JEFF MOYE WAS THE CONSUMMATE high achiever. He lived in Deadwood, South Dakota, where he had been a three-time mayor, president of the Chamber of Commerce, Chairman of the Board of the local museum, police commissioner, manager of the public utility company, head of the water sanitation district, and even Grand Exalted Ruler of the B.P.O.E. Almost everyone in town knew and liked him because of his positive attitude and terrific sense of humor. When Jeff died, the local newspaper planned to run a lengthy obituary citing his many achievements. But Jeff had decided he wanted to get one last chuckle out of his friends.

When Jeff's son, John, arrived in town to handle his father's funeral arrangements, he found a note instructing him to cancel the planned obituary. At Jeff's direction, in the newspaper's obit column the next morning his friends read, "Jeff Moye left town yesterday. He is not expected to return."

How creative—and how telling! This small vignette from Jeff's life speaks volumes about who he was, how he approached life, and how he wanted to leave his friends on a note of joy instead of sadness. We don't know if Jeff died with a smile on his face, but it's a good bet that he felt fulfillment in his heart.

In this book, we have defined happiness as a state of joy and well-being. Fulfillment is a state of satisfaction that is achieved when we are proud of ourselves, committed to personal growth, and know that our lives have value. Virtually everyone wants happiness in their lives. But not everyone will expend the extra energy required to achieve fulfillment. As Michael Stein observed, some people are content with tranquility and inner peace. There is absolutely nothing wrong with that. We each have the right to determine what we want from life. And a successful retirement is one in which we achieve the level of long-lasting happiness and fulfillment we desire.

Solving the Retirement Puzzle, however, is for the people who are driven to go beyond happiness to fulfillment. This chapter addresses what you can do to reach your own personally defined objectives. First, there is a self-analysis technique that will help you evaluate your relative happiness and fulfillment. The strategies you can follow to get the most out of the rest of your life are then discussed.

The Retirement Satisfaction Continuum

EVERY RETIREE FITS SOMEWHERE on the Retirement Satisfaction Continuum, graphically illustrated below:

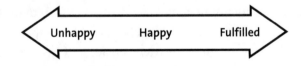

Most people find happiness in retirement and some find fulfillment. Others are less fortunate. Remember Tip Anderson?

Tip was the attorney-turned-businessman who ran into financial problems after he sold his business and it failed. Although he is in good health, Tip confided that he spends his time fighting off the demons of failure, worrying about finances, and trying to salvage his life. His relationship with his wife is strained, he doesn't have many personal friends, and he doesn't see anything to be enthusiastic about. Tip finds himself in the unfortunate position of being mired near the left end of the Retirement Satisfaction Continuum.

By contrast, Carol Grever—like most of the people in the Retirement Puzzle Cohort—indicated that she is comfortably situated closer to the right end of the continuum. Carol related how she overcame the anguish of her husband's disclosure that he was gay. She faced extreme stress and had to recreate her identity, which included reevaluating her spiritual beliefs. But having done so, she reported that she now feels good about her life. She has a sense of meaning and purpose, is in a loving long-term relationship, can't think of anything that she would change, and doesn't know anyone else who is as lucky as she. What a transformation!

As observed earlier, your success in retirement will not be determined by the problems you face. That is something over which you have little or no control. Your success, instead, will be determined by your mindset—how you approach life and deal with the problems you face. Your mindset is one thing that you can control.

The chart on pages 200–201 shows how people occupying different positions along the Retirement Satisfaction Continuum typically manage the major issues they face in retirement. Take a few minutes to determine where you are positioned on the chart.

As is suggested by the chart, people who are unhappy generally have little self-confidence, tend to believe that they are at the

The Retirement Satisfaction Continuum
Issues Analysis*

RETIREMENT ISSUES	UNHAPPY
Approach to Life	Pessimistic
Financial Status and Management	Insecure and undisciplined
Physical Health	Unhealthy and/or uncommitted to health maintenance
Mental Health	Impaired and disconnected, possibly depressed
Spirituality	Undeveloped and disinterested
Relationships	Incomplete and transitory
Self-Esteem	Poor

*Establish your level of satisfaction by assessing your management of the primary issues faced in retirement. It is unlikely that all of your rankings will be grouped exclusively under one of the headings—unhappy, happy, or fulfilled. You should, however, be able to approximate where you currently are positioned on the continuum.

HAPPY	FULFILLED
Optimistic	Optimistic, balanced with realism
Comfortable and responsible	Secure and responsible
Healthy and/or engaged in health maintenance	Healthy and/or committed to health maintenance
Aware and connected, wholesome	Vigorous, connected, and stimulated
Developed and resolute	Developed and ever-growing
Complete and lasting	Complete, lasting, and selfless
Self-confident	Self-confident and insightful

mercy of forces beyond their influence, and are passive when it comes to making changes in their lives. People who are happy are more optimistic, more engaged in life, and more comfortable with the way that their lives are unfolding. Those who feel fulfilled look favorably on their lives as well, but they have an additional drive to keep growing and expanding their horizons. They abhor the thought of stagnating or allowing their lives to drift.

It is natural for people to want to improve their lives by finding greater happiness and fulfillment — by shifting their focus somewhat to the right on the Retirement Satisfaction Continuum. However, doing so is not easy. It takes energy and commitment to reposition yourself. But, if you do want to make changes — if you want to find happiness *and* fulfillment — there are three strategies revealed by the Retirement Puzzle Cohort that will allow you to accomplish your goals. These are discussed in the following sections.

If Your Future is Your Past, You're History

BENJAMIN FRANKLIN WAS MISTAKEN when he said that nothing is certain but death and taxes. Change is also inevitable. In the years ahead, your world will change and you will have to change with it. There will be changes in your relationships with friends and relatives, changes in your body, changes in your physical abilities, and other changes you cannot anticipate. To have a successful retirement, you must adapt appropriately.

T. J. Levitt, who was so lost when he entered retirement that he started drinking around the clock, learned an important lesson. "What I learned is that you shouldn't retire until you have finished your journey in the workplace. And when you do finish that journey, you should unpack and prepare yourself for the next journey. That's a real process. You have to look back and understand where you've been, but you also have to go through the mental exercise of setting new goals and realistic expectations for the future."

Planning is helpful, but it is not enough. While adaptation is essential during the first days of retirement, it remains crucial throughout the retirement years. The problems you will face will rarely be the problems you considered or foresaw. You will have to adapt to meet changing circumstances. Some suggestions:

- When you retire, retire *to* something not *away* from something

- Let go of old expectations

- Live within your means

- Don't hide in the past or repeatedly tell old stories

- Stay aware of and take interest in what is going on around you

- Expect change

Vibrant retirees are able to put the past behind them and live in the present.

They also are self-aware. Bob Atchley, who has spent so many years studying and working with seniors, observed that the people who are happiest and most fulfilled in retirement "have self-knowledge and self-acceptance. They are the people who have done their homework on themselves." They see life as it is, not how they would like it to be. To improve your own perspective:

- Know your strengths and interests

- Accept reality, including your shortcomings

- Develop a personal philosophy through which you relate to the world around you

- Discover and maintain a spiritual connection that puts your life in perspective

- Set personal goals that are attainable

To adapt appropriately to the changes you will encounter, you must know who you are and be true to your values.

Another aspect of adaptability is commitment to personal growth. As Shari Ulrich, the former flight attendant with six college degrees said, "It's always nice to be around people who are excited about life and what they do — and who are challenged by it." The keys are to focus on doing what you enjoy, stimulate your mind, and always be on a learning curve. The closer you come to approaching your potential, the more fulfilled you will feel.

Moving beyond the past and embracing the present are important steps toward finding happiness and fulfillment. Thus, being adaptable is the first of the three strategies you can use to achieve your goals.

You Can Choose to be Happy – and Fulfilled

BOB ATCHLEY CALLS RETIREMENT a "do-it-yourself project." Just as nobody else can make you happy, nobody else can make you fulfilled. It's up to you to create your dreams. And you are the only one who can make them come true.

Choosing to be positive is one of the most important decisions you can make. For some people it is natural. For others it is difficult. But for everyone it is crucial. Mary Ide told us that she suffered from anxiety attacks. She was afraid to go out and afraid to stay home. With a lot of effort and assistance she was able to overcome her fears, but only after she changed her attitude. "It was a hard two years, but I finally learned that the solution has to be internal. You have to realize that nobody else is going to change your life for you. You have to develop a positive attitude and let it grow. You have to understand that you will only get as much out of life as you are willing to put in."

The benefits of a positive approach to life are miraculous: lower stress, improved immune systems, better health, greater self-confidence, stronger relationships, more happiness, and longer lives. A positive attitude can be a self-fulfilling prophecy because expectations often alter outcomes.

Positive people tend to adapt well to change. Because of their self-confidence, they are not overly concerned about what other people think, and they are more willing to make decisions on their own terms. With their heightened capacity for joy and laughter, they are inclined to live in the present rather than hang on to the past. And since they are less fearful of the future than those who are not positive, they are better able to cope with the indignities of aging.

Positive people are also much less likely to tire of life. As Peggy Becker said after the death of her husband and two broken hips, "The bad things in life aren't just going to happen to other people. They can happen to you, but you need to have the right attitude. I may have broken two hips and they may hurt, but they aren't going to keep me from living my life. I'm going to walk without that walker."

Becoming positive is a watershed decision — and staying positive is crucial to finding happiness and fulfillment. The following suggestions may help:

- Remember to be grateful. Thank the people who help make your life worthwhile.

- Practice forgiveness. When you hold on to bitterness about earlier events in your life, you are only hurting yourself. As Carol Grever said, "It's like eating rat poison and expecting the rat to die."

- Avoid self-indulgence. If you retire and lead a life of self-indulgence, you will become bored and then boring. Thinking beyond yourself fosters positive energy.

- Adapt your expectations to your reality. Hanging on to infeasible expectations — whether social, financial, or health-related — is one of the greatest sources of unhappiness.

- Live each day fully. Focus on staying involved in the activities that most interest you. Be pro-active.

- Use your strengths and avoid dwelling on your shortcomings. Everyone feels better about themselves when they feel competent.

- Enjoy life. Avoid taking yourself too seriously and remember to laugh.

The benefits of living with a positive attitude cannot be overstated. This does not mean that you should become blindly optimistic. Fulfillment comes to those who can balance their overall positive approach to life with a firm grip on reality.

You Have to Live to Have a Life

BEING ADAPTABLE AND POSITIVE are giant steps in the "right" direction. But they alone will not lead to happiness and fulfillment. The third strategy is to stay involved.

Some people dream and plan but fail to act. Others, like David Jackson, understand that you have to live to have a life. David wanted to learn about other people and how they live. So each year he embarked on a new adventure, like traveling on a Mississippi River barge, picking peaches, living with the

Hutterites and Amish, or traveling with a circus. Yes, actions do speak louder than words, but David's words capture his vitality. "You want to end up saying, 'I'm glad I did' rather than 'I wish I had.'"

David's approach to life reflects an interesting dichotomy that exists in people who thrive through retirement into old age. His passion for freedom and independence is mixed with an equally strong drive to be socially aware and involved. You will find greater happiness and fulfillment if you are friendly and socially engaged.

One of the clearest messages from the Retirement Puzzle Cohort is that the people who are closest to you are your most important treasures. Mary Elliott said, "Having money and having your health are both important, but nothing is more important than having relationships with people who you love and who love you back." Jo Kearney found that friends "give me a carefree, joyous connection. There is camaraderie, trust, and a sharing of life's experiences without any expectations. Being with them is a total release from everything else that goes on in my life. In so many ways, life is fulfilling if you can have a handful of friends that you can trust."

Nevertheless, as Neil Rosenthal pointed out, there is more to life than being connected to your family and friends. "Intimate relationships are one key—but not the only key—to having a full life. Simply having intimate relationships is not enough. We need more in our lives. We need to have goals to shoot for. We need to have things to do. We need to feel productive. These can be whatever we choose, as long as they keep us motivated and involved."

One of the truly great opportunities for staying involved during our retirement years is to give to others. Helping other people—by volunteering, mentoring, role modeling, making financial contributions, or just listening—leads directly to happiness and fulfillment. Thus, giving is the grandest form of selfishness. It brings satisfaction that cannot be duplicated in any other way. As Ken Pinson, who volunteers to support lonely senior men, said, "When we listen to other people, when we begin to think about someone other than ourselves, when we show concern for something other than our own problems, we become more engaged. And that makes our own lives better."

Staying engaged in life—staying involved with people and the world around you—is the essence of living.

The Foundation for a Successful Retirement

BY BECOMING ADAPTABLE, positive, and involved, you develop the attitudinal foundation for a successful retirement. These also are the qualities needed to cope with the major challenges you face in retirement. To find happiness and fulfillment, it is important to (1) prepare financially, (2) make a proper transition, (3) manage your physical, mental, and spiritual health, (4) revitalize your relationships, and (5) maintain your self-esteem. Clearly, your chance of having a successful retirement will be best if you properly deal with all of these challenges.

My research into *Solving the Retirement Puzzle* led to some other observations you may want to consider:

- I learned that the people who believe a successful retirement requires robust health and wealth are wrong. Some people thrive in retirement despite wrestling with health and financial issues. And there are healthy and wealthy people who are very unhappy and unfulfilled— even depressed. Close personal relationships and self-esteem are at least as important as health and wealth if you hope to achieve happiness and fulfillment.

- Change is inevitable as you proceed through the three phases of retirement. Your energy and health will probably be much better early on. Those are precious commodities. Take advantage of them while you have them.

■ The people who are most likely to achieve happiness *and* fulfillment are committed to lifelong learning. It is important to be open to new ideas and new experiences and not allow yourself to be trapped in outdated thinking. Every person and experience you have has the potential to be a teacher that helps you grow.

■ Over time, you will need to adapt to a more sedentary lifestyle. Unfortunately, some people view this phase of life as one encumbered by devastating limitations. Your life will improve greatly if you instead look for opportunities to recreate yourself. It is a time to use your mind, capitalize on your experience, and share with the people around you. Be prepared to deal with the changes that are unavoidable.

■ Your chances of having a successful retirement and coping with the changes that aging brings will increase if you have a strong spiritual connection. It is wise to keep everything in perspective. If you have not done so already, now is a good time to take your spiritual journey.

■ In retirement, having passion is the difference between being occupied and being exhilarated. When we are committed to something and we challenge ourselves — particularly when we reach out to others — we have a sense of meaning and purpose that leads to fulfillment.

■ There will always be opportunities to be a contributing member of your community. As Mike Sargent said, "You spend the first half of your life seeking success and should spend the second half seeking significance." Bob Atchley added that the people who help and support others receive much more back in return. "The break-through happens when the action of service, in and of itself, becomes rewarding. That is when people feel truly joyful and appreciative and awed about where they are in their lives. They have gone beyond that materialistic place and are able to see life in a very different way." Growing old is not easy, but it can be done gracefully.

Midge's Prayer

WHEN WE WERE YOUNG, we were driven by our dreams and aspirations. We were energized by the challenges we faced, and we reveled in the satisfaction, recognition, and sense of control that resulted from our accomplishments. For many of us, the accumulation of material objects was an important measure of success. Together, these factors played important roles in shaping and reinforcing our identities, and they gave us confidence in a world of expanding opportunities.

Retirement is a different world in which identifying and pursuing new challenges, making contributions to our friends, family, and community, and maintaining close personal relationships become increasingly important. Accumulating material objects decreases in relevance. At this stage of our lives, it is usually from human interactions that we find our greatest sense of satisfaction.

One of the keys to happiness and fulfillment is to know who we are and where we are in the life cycle. Midge Bartlett was well into her nineties when she died. After her death, her son found the following prayer among her personal belongings. I'll leave the last word to her.

*Lord, Thou know better than I know myself
that I am growing older and will, some day, be very old.*

*Keep me from getting talkative
and particularly from the fatal habit of thinking
that I must say something on every subject
and on every occasion.*

*Release me from craving to straighten out everybody's affairs.
Keep me from the recital of endless details.
Help me to come to the point.*

*I ask for grace enough to listen to the tales of others' pains.
Help me to endure them with patience.*

*But seal my lips concerning my own aches and pains.
They are increasing and my love of discussing them
becomes sweeter as the years go by.*

*Teach me the glorious lesson that occasionally
it is possible that I may be mistaken.
Keep me reasonably sweet.
I don't want to be a saint.
Some of them are so hard to live with;
but a sour old woman is one of the crowning works of the devil.*

*Make me thoughtful but not moody; helpful but not bossy.
With my vast store of wisdom it seems a pity not to use it all.
But Thou knowest I want a few friends at the end.*

Thoughts for Retirees from Famous People

I have found the best way to give advice to your children is to find out what they want and then advise them to do it.

—HARRY S. TRUMAN

Anyone who stops learning is old, whether at twenty or eighty. Anyone who keeps learning stays young. The greatest thing in life is to keep your mind young.　　　　　—HENRY FORD

Life was meant to be lived, and curiosity must be kept alive. One must never, for whatever reason, turn his back on life.

—ELEANOR ROOSEVELT

The man who views the world at fifty the same as he did at twenty has wasted thirty years of his life.　　　—MUHAMMAD ALI

I thank God for my handicaps, for through them, I have found myself, my work, and my God.　　　—HELEN KELLER

You can make more friends in two months by becoming interested in other people than you can in two years by trying to get other people interested in you.　　　—DALE CARNEGIE

Old age is like a plane flying through a storm. Once you're aboard, there's nothing you can do.　　　—GOLDA MEIR

I want to die in my sleep like my grandfather. Not screaming and yelling like the passengers in his car.　　　—EMO PHILLIPS

If something comes to life in others because of you, then you have made an approach to immortality.　　　—NORMAN COUSINS

Become a possibilitarian. No matter how dark things seem to be or actually are, raise your sights and see possibilities. Always see them, for they are always there.   —NORMAN VINCENT PEALE

Solitude is painful when one is young, but delightful when one is more mature.   —ALBERT EINSTEIN

Love . . . is perhaps the only glimpse we are permitted of eternity.
          —HELEN HAYES

When you become senile, you won't know it.
          —BILL COSBY

There is no higher religion than human service. To work for the common good is the greatest creed.   —ALBERT SCHWEITZER

Happiness lies in the joy of achievement and the thrill of creative effort.   —FRANKLIN D. ROOSEVELT

An archeologist is the best husband any woman can have: The older she gets, the more interested he is in her.   —AGATHA CHRISTIE

Satisfaction lies in the effort, not in the attainment. Full effort is full victory.   —MAHATMA GANDHI

You are unique, and if that is not fulfilled, then something has been lost.   —MARTHA GRAHAM

Old age isn't so bad when you consider the alternative.
          —MAURICE CHEVALIER

There is nothing more tragic than to find an individual bogged down in the length of life, devoid of breadth.
          —MARTIN LUTHER KING JR.

To me, old age is always fifteen years older than I am.
          —BERNARD BARUCH

I don't believe in dying. It's been done. I'm working on a new exit.
          —GEORGE BURNS

Acknowledgements

ONE OF THE GREAT LESSONS I LEARNED from researching this book is that people who have lived long, productive lives have an incredible wealth of knowledge, experience, and common sense that is undervalued, even dismissed by society. I thank everyone who was willing to share their life stories and sage advice. Although the comments of only forty of them are included in the book, many others greatly helped me understand the retirement issues that people face.

Denis Nock and Mike Sargent, two members of the Retirement Puzzle Cohort, were especially helpful in monitoring my progress and providing suggestions. A special thanks goes to both of them for helping me develop my thoughts and observations.

Lyn McQueen and Lynne Foley are on the staff at Frasier Meadows Manor, a continuous care community in Boulder, Colorado. Both were very helpful in guiding me to information about retirement and aging. And through their networks they led me to several of the people in the Retirement Puzzle Cohort.

Finally, I have a very special thanks to my wife and daughter. Gayla offered many valuable suggestions—particularly those that added a woman's perspective. Thank you, Gayla, for your insights and your tolerance during my obsession with this project. Brooke spent endless hours editing and bringing greater clarity and cohesion to the book. She also reinforced the women's perspective. Brooke, thank you for your perception and diligence. You two have made this ride all the more enjoyable.

About the Author

PETE LINDQUIST grew up in Michigan and Colorado. In 1984, he founded Quist Financial, Inc. (now Quist Valuation, Inc.), which became the leading valuation and securities analysis company in the Rocky Mountain region. The firm helped clients prepare for retirement by selling family businesses, valuing companies and investments, and providing planning and related financial consulting services. After selling his company and retiring in 2002, Pete became more interested in the non-financial aspects of retirement. He set out on a journey to determine what people could do to find happiness and fulfillment during their retirement years. This book is the result of that inquiry. Pete's wife, Gayla, is a retired school principal. They have two grown children who live nearby in the Denver metropolitan area.

The Retirement Puzzle College

IF YOU READ THIS BOOK and learned how to improve your retirement experience, you have successfully fulfilled the requirements for an honorary DOCTOR OF RETIREMENT SCIENCES diploma from The Retirement Puzzle College. To receive your personalized diploma, go to www.lifepuzzles.org and e-mail us your comments and suggestions. Upon receipt of your email your diploma will be sent to you.

Notes